Praise for *Why Study Language*

T0169919

I defy anyone to read this book and not end up passionate about the importance and the pleasure of languages. With a combination of research, statistics, anecdotes and human interest stories and interviews, it is precisely targeted to its main audience of prospective students and their parents. If you still believe that English is enough, prepare to be disabused!

Baroness Jean Coussins, Vice-President, Chartered Institute of Linguists, Co-Chair, All Party Parliamentary Group on Modern Languages, President, Speak to the Future Campaign

Why Study Languages? is as rich in information as it is in experience. It will answer your questions about the nature of languages and communication, dispel many negative myths about language learning, and provide evidence that studying languages is not only useful but also rewarding, exhilarating and, often, life-changing.

Loredana Polezzi, Alfonse M. D'Amato Chair in Italian American and Italian Studies, Stony Brook University

A valuable insight into the myriad of ways in which the study of languages can enrich our experience of the world, be that personal or professional.

Catriona Kyle, assistant headteacher, Channing School, London

Join Gabrielle Hogan-Brun on a voyage of discovery around the wonderful world of languages. You will meet a crowd of fascinating people and hear how languages have enriched their lives. You might even want to follow them and put yourself at the centre of a new map.

Michael Kelly, Emeritus Professor of French, University of Southampton

In this great new book – one filled with inspiration and pragmatism – Gabrielle Hogan-Brun shows you how languages have the power to shape your life. You'll find real-life stories of both ordinary and famous people. You'll see how knowing languages helped them to become successful and to find their place in the world. You'll read about careers you might want to consider with languages. And you'll also learn how you can get started – and where. If you are wondering whether studying languages is the right path for you, this comprehensive and easy-to-follow guide will help you decide. I hope your answer will be a yes!

Gabriella Ferenczi, German and Hungarian language coach,
founder of ProLingua Global

If you'd like to become a global citizen, being able to navigate the pathways that language study leads to is essential. This book will provide the support you'll need to fulfil that aim. The book sets out the practical realities, the available resources, the societal needs and the range of opportunities that are open to you. I recommend you draw on Gabrielle Hogan-Brun's tips to give you the motivation for sustained language learning that will provide you with a 'healthy linguistic diet'!

Maria K. Norton, Deputy Director International Relations,
University of Southampton

WHY STUDY LANGUAGES?

The *Why Study* Series

Studying any subject at degree level is an investment in the future that involves significant cost. Now more than ever, students and their parents need to weigh up the potential benefits of university courses. That's where the *Why Study* series comes in. This series of books, aimed at students, parents and teachers, explains in practical terms the range and scope of an academic subject at university level and where it can lead in terms of careers or further study. Each book sets out to enthuse the reader about its subject and answer the crucial questions that a college prospectus does not.

Published

Why Study History? — Marcus Collins and Peter N. Stearns
Why Study Mathematics? — Vicky Neale
Why Study Geography? — Alan Parkinson
Why Study Languages? — Gabrielle Hogan-Brun

WHY STUDY LANGUAGES?

BY GABRIELLE HOGAN-BRUN

Published by London Publishing Partnership
www.londonpublishingpartnership.co.uk

All Rights Reserved

ISBN: 978-1-913019-18-1 (pbk)

A catalogue record for this book is available from the British Library

This book has been composed in Kepler Std

Copy-edited and typeset by T&T Productions Ltd, London
www.tandtproductions.com

Printed and bound in Great Britain by Page Bros

Cover image

Spices from Asia and Africa were in great demand in Medieval Europe, and many cities and individuals were made very rich indeed through their links with the spice trade. Pepper, cinnamon, nutmeg, cloves and many other exotic flavourings were used in medicine and cosmetics as well as in food and wine. Traders were practical and used different languages to obtain these precious resources from faraway places. And the modern world is no different: language skills are just as highly valued as the commodities and services we require from around the globe, and they're seen not only as a way of embracing diversity but also as a resource to enhance business and cooperation and increase our knowledge of the world. Another language will surely add spice to your life.

CONTENTS

For Patrick & Justine, Sarah & Giles, Christopher & Nalinie

PREFACE:
WHY THIS BOOK?

Are you *interested in* languages but maybe not so sure that you want to *study* them? You've come to the right place.

This book explains what languages are about: their excitements, their challenges, the skills they provide and what you can do with them. You'll hear from students, from professionals and from famous names who learned languages at school, at university and beyond. Their personal anecdotes bear testimony to the real difference that studying languages has made to their lives.

This book is intended as an accessible and essential guide to why you should consider studying languages, and to how and where you can do so. Throughout, I've avoided concerning myself with the technicalities of learning and have instead adopted a holistic perspective, focusing my attention on you as a learner. While you read, you may find yourself reflecting on what type of person you are. What are your ambitions? What do you want out of life? Where are you planning to go? What drives your interest in languages?

You'll find answers to many practical questions in the chapters that follow. How do you choose which course to take, and which language to study? How might you go about funding your education? What career opportunities will the study of languages provide you with? What's your earning potential? What can languages do for you as you move through life? You'll discover that, as well as supporting your personal and working life, languages also promote cultural understanding and social cohesion.

The core message of *Why Study Languages?* is that learning a language is beneficial for anyone, at any age. Languages are all around us and are used in all walks of life. Language diversity is a fact of everyday experience, whether offline or online. If you speak only one language, you risk being left out of the conversation.

ACKNOWLEDGEMENTS

Many thanks go to Richard Baggaley, Sam Clark and Ellen White at London Publishing Partnership, and to three anonymous reviewers.

I am grateful to my husband, John, for his generous support and loving care. This book is dedicated to our children and to their partners, all of whom have embraced their multilingual relationships, seeing with their own eyes the benefits of knowing other cultures.

WHY STUDY LANGUAGES?

CHAPTER 1

Why study languages?

By picking up this book, you've shown that you're curious: you want to know more about the world and you're eager to learn about what's beyond your immediate horizon. You're wondering whether learning another language might help you to stretch your wings. Perhaps you're also wondering whether you have the necessary skills to study languages.

In fact, you're already a language expert! You've absorbed your childhood language(s) with ease. You can speak and understand your language(s)[1] and are continually developing these skills. You have what it takes and you're ready to learn another.

Maybe you already have an idea of which language might interest you. Perhaps it's Portuguese, because that's your dad's native language. Perhaps it's Russian, because your heart beats faster every time you hear it spoken. For most people, their first idea is the one to go for: follow that instinct and you'll do well.

There are usually three significant waypoints in your life at which you can decide to study a language. The first comes at school, where you should be offered the opportunity to learn at least one language up to the age of 18. Then, at university, you can study one or more languages in depth, or you can combine your language course with a completely different subject (German with mathematics, for example). You can also take up a language as an optional module. And third, you might decide to learn a language once you've left full-time education, or at some later stage of life.

While I will discuss each of these cases in this book, my main focus will be on university choices. There's a good reason for this. Choosing your degree subject is probably one of the biggest decisions you'll make in life (up there with whether to get married, buy a house, have children, etc.). You'll need to think not only about what to study, but also about where to study. And then you'll have to find out about funding to finance your choice as well. Maybe someone has advised you to do something 'useful' at university. Maybe you have no idea what you want to do when you graduate. Will you make the right choice?

As a young person trying to find answers to the question posed by this book's title, you'll be encouraged by some people. But from others you might hear: 'Why bother? Everyone speaks English anyway!' (In reality, only about 20% of the world's population speaks English, and for most it's a second language.) You might also be warned that you'll need a 'gift for languages', when you don't actually need any such special talent.

Part of the conundrum with languages is that they're simultaneously everywhere and nowhere. You'll go abroad and find that everyone speaks another language. Yet back home, despite the government having a Chief Scientific Advisor, a Chief Medical Officer and even a Chief Mathematician, there's no Chief Linguist. And there are few gripping movies in which the hero or heroine is a linguist.[2] Unlike, say, a law firm, you won't be able to find a local languages firm where you can do a week's work experience. Is learning a language really worth the effort?

This book will demonstrate that it is. It will give you the facts about the personal and financial gains from doing so, and it will tell you about the social benefits of knowing multiple languages. Speaking through the voices of individuals from different walks of life, it will show you how being skilled in languages is useful, enriching and valuable. When you've finished reading, you'll be able to make an informed decision about learning languages.

Studying languages at A level

At school, you can choose to study at least one language alongside other subjects up to the age of 18. You're likely to find the available language options limited, depending on where you're taught, but as you'll see in a moment, that shouldn't restrict your choices at university (you can nearly always study a language from scratch there, if you like).

All schools will lay out the reasons for studying the particular language(s) they offer. For example, here's what Ashbourne College in London has to say about opting for a French A level:

> *French is one of the most widely learned languages in the world and spoken by more than 200 million people in four different continents – so you will be in good company.*
>
> *Being able to speak French will allow you to work for some of the world's major organizations in which French is an official language including the United Nations, the European Union, UNESCO, NATO, the World Trade Organization and the International Red Cross.*[3]

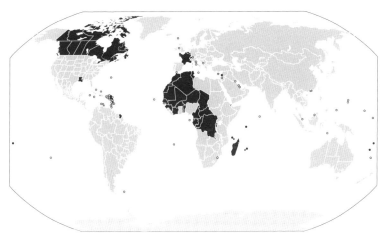

Figure 1 French has official status in twenty-nine countries across the globe. The majority of speakers are in Europe, Africa and Canada, and there are pockets of speakers in the West Indies, in parts of Asia and in the Middle East. (Figure adapted from original image found on Wikimedia Commons.)

The course outline goes on to list the many fields in which French-speaking companies operate, such as 'media, finance, industry, tourism and sport'. It also insists you'll be 'well catered for' if you have an interest in 'cooking, fashion, arts, dance and architecture'. It proposes that learning French helps 'improve your communication and critical thinking skills' and that this will have 'a positive impact on other studies'. Finally, it says that knowing French makes it 'easier to learn other Romance-based languages like Spanish, Italian and Portuguese'.

The description above captures some of the themes I'll develop in this book: namely, that studying a language will help you to communicate with lots of different people from diverse backgrounds, to get a job in a range of industries, and to acquire many transferable skills. It's also true that mastering one language is often a gateway to learning others.

Some schools will use personal experiences from trips their pupils have taken to convince you to learn languages. Here's what one student from Liverpool College had to say about his sixth-form trip to Seville in Spain:[4]

> *We headed out early to Torre del Oro, a military watchtower from the thirteenth century which had amazing views overlooking the River Guadalquivir. We took time to look around its Naval Museum at the top of the tower before then heading to another famous landmark, El Alcázar.*

The student goes on to explain how fascinating it was to see with his own eyes the 'Arabic-inspired architectural features' of this fortress. Another highlight of the trip was a visit to Seville Cathedral, which is the largest in Spain.

So many lines of enquiry, spanning hundreds of years, arise from this simple description. I'm sure the teacher in charge would have asked their students lots of questions about the new cultural experiences they were encountering. What was Torre del Oro defending? What happened to the people who built El Alcázar?

How and when did the country shift from Islam to Catholicism? Here we have another theme of this book: languages as a door to other cultures.

Studying languages at university

Once you've studied a language at school, you may be tempted to continue or expand on your learning at university. But where, and how? A good place to start would be to ask some students who are already at university. There will be almost as many answers as students, of course, but below are some examples to give you a flavour of what people are saying.

First up is James Freeman, who's studying Italian and Portuguese at the University of Bristol.[5] By choosing this (less common) language combination, James is putting into practice what we read earlier: that it's easier to learn related languages.

Having studied French and Italian at A-level, I decided to continue with Italian as I had done French for seven years at that point, and then, of the new languages that were available to me, Portuguese made the most sense. It's widely spoken and is a Romance language, so I already had a good foundation.

James isn't concentrating solely on his language skills through his Bachelor of Arts (BA), either: he's also keen to learn about cultural production in the languages he's studying. Among the wide variety of units offered, he picked both classical literature (including the work of Dante) and modern gangster films.

James also seized the opportunity to do a year abroad, in order to immerse himself in the environments of his chosen languages. He decided to work, rather than study, in Trieste (Northern Italy) and in Salvador (Brazil):

I was slightly worried that it might be harder socially, given that I wouldn't be studying, but I still met lots of students, and if anything, it just meant that I met lots of people I wouldn't have met had I just been at university.

James is using the opportunities provided by his languages degree to face new challenges, encounter new people and get to know new cultures. His experience is a real-life manifestation of the prospects mentioned by Ashbourne College that we saw earlier. They're not just possibilities, now: they're a reality.

Is James's experience typical? Here's Evangeline Henry, who's doing a BA in French at University College London (UCL).[6] She chose to study modern francophone literature, including that of Algeria and Haiti. As part of her final year, she even took a module on Tintin. Evangeline's experience is proof that even if you focus on a single language at university, your studies can span continents. And you don't have to just cover the classics: even comics are allowed!

Evangeline also learned important social and personal skills on her course:

Studying French … has given me a lot more than French skills because life is not learnt, contrary to what I thought before starting, from a textbook. It taught me resilience, determination, how to adjust quickly to new situations, what to do when things go wrong and how to celebrate when they go right.

Like James, she applied for a work placement abroad:

My internship not only improved my language, but also gave me the chance to explore my creativity and discover a new industry: learning marketing on the job was an excellent experience.

The professional insights Evangeline gained during her placement will be a huge advantage when she applies for a job. In Chapter 5 we'll meet Lucy Jeynes, whose career as a business executive attests to the benefits of doing a languages degree: doing so both instilled cultural insights and also enhanced Lucy's dexterity with English, her primary language.

Now let's meet Anthony Fairclough, who's doing a combined German Studies and Politics degree at Lancaster University.[7] He originally intended to study Politics and International Relations but then opted to add German as a minor, and he hasn't looked back since. In Anthony's own words, his degree choice has afforded 'so many opportunities that I would never have known about', including the possibility of an internship in Germany:

Figure 2   On 9 November 1989, citizens of the GDR were free to cross the country's borders. The reunification of East and West Germany was made official almost a year after the fall of the Berlin Wall. (This file is licensed under the Creative Commons Attribution-Share Alike 3.0 Unported license.)

I worked in Germany for a year, gaining employability and life experience, as well as developing my confidence. I also made good friends and now the town in Germany feels a little like home. ... Coming from being a complete beginner, the department taught me not only the language but also the importance of culture. One of the standout modules for me ... focused on German politics and history since 1945, which also helped with my politics modules.

Anthony goes on to talk about gaining an understanding of German culture. But he's not talking about art or literature, as you might expect, or about culture in the sense of ruins, towers, battles or cathedrals. Instead, he's been able to connect his insights into the German language with living, breathing politics that has happened during our lifetimes and those of our parents. Paradoxically, perhaps, this experience has probably helped Anthony to understand his own culture better too.

But what if you want to study another subject and take a language as an option rather than as the main focus of your degree? Here's Jason Valdes, a Kenpo karate instructor. He's interested in Japanese culture, which heavily influenced his form of martial arts. Now a student at the University of Rhode Island (URI), Jason's final year will find him studying in Japan. In an interview with the writer Neil Nachbar, he explained:[8]

I heard some great things about the International Engineering Program (IEP) when I was in high school. Since [URI's IEP] offered a Japanese track, I thought it would be a great opportunity to learn the Japanese language and share the Japanese culture with others.

He's already planning to put both his engineering skills and his passion for karate – enhanced by his deeper experience of Japanese language and culture – to good use after graduation. He hopes to find a job in Japan as a technical liaison or as engineering support for products sold there, teaching karate in his spare time.

Reasons to study languages

As you may have gathered, these students had a strong internal drive to embark on their language journey, and this drive has taken them places. In the same way, having an awareness of your own abilities and desires will put you on the path to making good decisions. From the accounts above, we can begin to discern what motivates people to study languages.

First, everyone we've already met decided that studying languages was a way to follow their passion. This is probably the clearest reason to study anything, so if this applies to you too, great! Why not enjoy yourself as you learn and gain skills? It was certainly true for James, from the University of Bristol, whom we met earlier. He had a love of Mediterranean (Romance) languages, and crucially – as with all the 'protagonists' you'll get to meet in this book – opting to study them presented him with fascinating and exciting opportunities.

You'll get to see what languages can do for you in Chapter 4. There, you'll meet Jhumpa Lahiri, a prize-winning American–Bangladeshi author, whose love affair with Italian enabled her to find fresh content for her writing. Similarly, Thomasina Miers – founder of the restaurant chain Wahaca and winner of the 2005 edition of the BBC's *MasterChef* – headed for Mexico after succumbing to the allure of the Spanish language. There, she found the inspiration that would come to shape her career as a chef. By following their dream to take up a new language, Jhumpa and Thomasina changed the course of their lives.

And there were other benefits, too. As Thomasina puts it, her decision to follow the calling of Spanish shaped her personally.

She felt she became partly Mexican in the process, as she began to appreciate the subtleties and idiosyncrasies of the language.[9] Her experience demonstrates that learning a language helps you to understand the fabric of a society: its culture and its traditions. In this case specifically, Thomasina discovered just how important food is to the Hispanic way of life.

So, culture covers all aspects of life: it can mean both cartoons *and* classical literature, as well as film, music, science and art. For James, the modules his university offered enabled him to delve deeper into the relationship between film, culture and society. For Anthony, at Lancaster University, learning about German culture through the German language gave him a better understanding of politics. And Jason's enthusiasm for karate while studying at URI made him want to find out how Japanese culture influenced this form of focused combat.

Equally important, perhaps, is the fact that learning about other cultures can open your eyes to the wider world. As you'll see in Chapter 4, BBC security correspondent Frank Gardner's fascination with Arabic unlocked a portal through which he could gain first-hand experience of life in the Middle East.[10] It enabled him to report from conflict zones across the Arab world.

We can also take another viewpoint: namely, that knowing a language can make things happen. Travel is perhaps the most obvious benefit of learning and using a language, as that sixth-form student from Liverpool College showed. And linked to travel is the fact that learning a language can help you make friends from totally different cultural backgrounds, which in turn gives you a deeper understanding of the world. It was during their time abroad that both James and Evangeline were able to try out careers in new industries, finding out what life might be like after graduation. In experiencing professional opportunities away from home, they found that their bilingual skills had utility in overseas markets.

This is especially the case when language ability comes hand-in-hand with other professional skills. For example, Jason's technical expertise in engineering combined with his knowledge of Japanese language and culture may well enable him to find employment in Japan or with an international organization closer to home. In Chapter 4 you'll also meet Matthias Maurer, whose tenacity with languages alongside his deep interest in science and technology allowed him to realize his dream of becoming an astronaut.

Admittedly, you may not see yourself following any of the above life trajectories. But each of the individuals we've met has gained in different ways from their language studies. Taking up another language meant they could speak with people from different countries, learn about the backgrounds of others, and discover new ways of seeing and doing things. Along the way, they have developed their social skills and gained a greater sense of cultural understanding and sensitivity, as well as deepening their empathy and their tolerance towards others.

Evidently, then, you can benefit in multiple ways from studying other languages. Like any mental activity, using more than one language exercises your brain. As you progress, you become more flexible at reasoning, which aids your personal development (see Chapter 3). Studying a language is even thought to lead to better overall health and well-being.

Moreover, as Evangeline found out, her period of immersion abroad made her stronger as a person. Language capability can equip you to deal with life's challenges better: an essential quality that's also valued by employers. And languages can also enhance your ability to act as a responsible citizen, supporting others by casually interpreting for them, in times of need. You'll meet Adul Sam-on in Chapter 4, whose facility with languages led to the dramatic rescue of him and his twelve friends from a flooded cave in Thailand in 2018.

As well as enhancing your critical thinking skills and your social competencies, learning another language will also help you become a more articulate and confident communicator. Not only will this shape your intercultural encounters, but it will also give you an advantage in education and employment. Especially when it is combined with 'hard' (or technical) skills, your knowledge of a different language will make a real difference to your future career (in economics or engineering, say) and will boost your employment opportunities both at home and abroad, and well beyond just language-based professions.

In discussing its French A level course, Ashbourne College gives many examples of careers – in industry, finance and the creative sector – where a knowledge of French is an advantage. The same is true of all languages. What's more, many companies now see multilanguage work teams as a major asset: one that fosters greater creativity. This is because each speaker comes with their own worldview and way of expressing things, which can be useful in developing new ideas for innovative solutions to practical problems.

To sum up what we've seen so far, the skills gained by learning languages are important in all forms of knowledge. They allow us to augment our intelligence. By studying a language you'll be exposed to a variety of cultures and different ways of life, so it follows that your language ability will lead to more opportunities and enhance personal growth, increasing your awareness and compassion. As active citizens in a globalized world, these are the tools we need to read, understand and debate the key issues that affect us all, every day.

Crucially, knowing languages is empowering. It's a skill that functions as an antidote to fake news and disinformation. It allows us to access evidence and analyse facts from multiple sources, in multiple languages, so that we can capture different points of view. All of this lessens the risk of content getting 'lost in translation'. Being able to retrieve information in different languages can be a means of getting 'under the skin' of news, and it can certainly help us to better understand what's going on in the world.

And finally ...

Languages touch all aspects of the human experience, and they serve as a fantastic springboard for personal development in all spheres of life and at any age. Deciding to become bilingual reflects the kind of person you want to be. It can mean reconfiguring how you think about communication, and putting yourself at the centre of a different map. It shows that you're prepared to play a role in promoting understanding across the globe as you develop into an articulate global citizen.

Learning a language has the potential to bring a greater sense of self-awareness into your life too. At its core, being bilingual means that you must invest your energy and time more purposefully. If at times you're moved to ask, in a bilingual context, 'is this really what I want to say?', you may begin to listen more carefully and become a more reflective person.

I hope this book will kindle your taste for languages and show you that learning another language is both practical and enriching. For sure, there is much more to it than textbook exercises and practice! In the end, though, only you can know whether studying languages is for you. In the next chapter we'll discover that for a high proportion of people around the globe it is quite normal to be multilingual, and we'll discuss how you too might benefit from knowing another language.

Jargon buster

You will come across many words to describe how many languages are spoken by whom and where: *monolingual, bilingual, trilingual, multilingual, plurilingual, polyglot, metrolingual,* to name but a few.

To keep things simple, I'll use *monolingual* to describe a person or (formally) society using only one language and *multilingual* to describe a person or society using more than one language (only occasionally, when the emphasis is firmly on two languages, will I choose the term *bilingual*).

Throughout the book I'll avoid the term *foreign languages*. This notion highlights the distance of others' ways of life and culture from our own, and in our world of heightened mobility and cultural mixing I see it as too fixed.

One final point: in educational settings, the term *modern languages* is often used to refer to languages that are still spoken. Instead, I'll just talk about 'languages' here, whether they are spoken today (yours or mine), widely used and learned (e.g. Spanish, Arabic) or not (e.g. Basque, Welsh), at risk (Cornish, among many), or still learned but no longer have their own community of native speakers (e.g. Latin, Ancient Greek).

CHAPTER 2

Just how multilingual are we?

MORE THAN 7,000 LANGUAGES ARE in use around the world today. For speakers from different language groups to communicate with one another, there must be some degree of multilingualism. In fact, as we shall see, these multilinguals are (almost) everywhere. So why is it that monolingualism is so much more prevalent in some societies than in others? And why are there so many languages in the first place?

You probably know individuals who manage to get by using just their own language. Many people remain monolingual because they don't have any social or economic incentives to learn another language. For example, in parts of rural England, away from the cities, being multilingual may reap no overt benefits. Almost everyone will speak English, and the few strangers who visit the UK's more remote areas will have picked up enough words of English to get by (or will carry a smartphone and be proficient at using Google Translate). If you only interact with people who share your language, you don't need to know another one.

One person who stands by his monolingual mindset is David, a teacher from Australia. He answered the question 'What does it feel like to speak and understand only one language?' (posed on the website Quora) with one word: 'consistent'.[11] It's not entirely clear what he had in mind when he formed that reply. Australia is home to a mosaic of different languages and the country has large, thriving Chinese, Vietnamese, Arabic, Greek and Italian communities, as well as more than 130 indigenous language groups. Some of these people may well be among David's pupils.

In this chapter, we're going to explore the use of languages around the globe, both now and in the distant past. We'll see that humans have always been resourceful in overcoming communication barriers. We'll learn that multilingualism is widespread and that, for huge sections of the world's population, knowing more than one language is commonplace. And, with you placed centre stage, we'll discover that languages are key for us all.

A monolingual perspective

Many people are content seeing their world from a monolingual perspective, even when they encounter speakers of other languages in their day-to-day lives. April, who lives in a part of the US that boasts vibrant Hispanic neighbourhoods, says she can use her native English with just about everyone around her. She's fine with having just one language. In response to the question 'What is it like to know just one language?' (also posted on Quora), April explains:

> *I'm an American. It hasn't really bugged me or held me back in my profession to only know one language. Most people here know some English. ... I guess there have been times I would enjoy being able to speak Spanish if I could. Not enough though to have to learn it.*[12]

In her post, April states that she feels kinship with her Hispanic American neighbours and likes their open, warm lifestyle. However, she finds that being monolingual doesn't greatly hinder her ability to appreciate this other culture. Can that really be true? Wouldn't learning Spanish help her to better understand the beliefs, customs and songs that inform her neighbours' way of life?

A knowledge of Spanish would no doubt enable April to also bond with many others from this background – those outside her immediate neighbourhood. After all, there are more than 52 million Spanish speakers in the US, making it the second most used language there, after English. Chinese is also widely spoken, as are French, Tagalog, Vietnamese, Korean and German. Multilinguals are found in all these language communities, with an uneven spread across the country.

In contrast with April, there are many US citizens who think that speaking and understanding only one language is a hindrance. Philipp, another Quora user, describes himself as someone who loves to learn, and he feels limited by his monolingualism:

You feel [fine] until you meet somebody who speaks more than one language. You feel [fine] until you can't take a trip to another country. You feel [fine] until your hopefully-soon-to-be-employer tells you that you need to know more than one language.[13]

For Philipp, monolingualism is restricting, in terms of both travel possibilities and career opportunities. He's aware of the benefits of knowing another language and is eager to reap them. This could well be the incentive that propels him to learn another language, to broaden his horizons and to find greater success in the job market.

April and Philipp are far from alone in being monolingual, of course. In fact, around 75% of US citizens (240 million people) speak only one language fluently; this compares with an estimated 40% of people globally.[14] Nevertheless, almost half the US population reportedly feels that it is important to have at least a basic grasp of another language, and awareness of existing bilingual capabilities as a countrywide resource is on the rise (see Figure 3).[15]

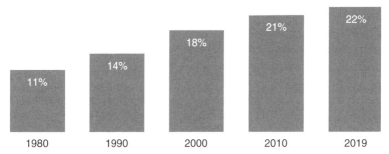

Figure 3 Percentage of US population who spoke a language other than English in their own home, by year. (*Source*: US Census Bureau American Community Survey (www.census.gov/programs-surveys/acs). Figure created by John Hogan.)

This appreciation is reflected in the country's business sector. According to a recent New American Economy press release, in the five years to 2017 the demand for bilingual workers has more than doubled, nationwide, across major industries,[16] and this trend is likely to continue. Spanish and Chinese are currently the most marketable second languages in the US, followed by Hindi, Russian, German and Portuguese.

This desire among companies to invest in staff with multilingual skills is not principally being driven by cultural shifts in the US. In fact, some of the top languages are those of cheap, highly skilled staff hired from outside by recruiters that are not widely spoken within the country. Instead, they reflect the international markets where these companies are keen to do business: South America, China, India, Russia, Germany and Brazil. We will return to this economic need for languages later.

Why this monolingualism?

Since our planet is home to speakers of thousands of different languages, how is it that monolingualism exists at all? Why is it that French is the official (national) language of France, Spanish of Spain and German of Germany? Is it *natural* for people to speak just one language?

There are many reasons for the persistence of monolingualism, but an important one is that languages spread with economic growth, and with economic growth come empires. This is not a modern phenomenon. When the Roman Empire was at its height in Europe, Latin and Greek were the de facto official languages: Latin was the language of administration, legislation and the military, while Greek was the language of high culture. Although local languages were tolerated, many imperial subjects chose to adopt Latin and Greek so they'd be accepted into society. The effects of this form of cultural expansion are still felt throughout the world today: many languages have, for instance, inherited words with roots in either Latin or Greek.

Once Europe's imperial powers had expanded their (mercantile) activities overseas – to the Americas, to Asia and to Australasia

– they exported their own languages too, which in time displaced the myriad other languages that already existed in these places. English took the lead as the language of wider communication among the big contenders (mainly French, Spanish, Portuguese, German and Russian). As was the case at the height of the Roman Empire, many people were attracted to learning these more widely used languages to increase their own chances of success and mobility. Slowly but surely, monolingualism started to develop. It even became a badge of social acceptability in some contexts.

At its core, the story of monolingualism is a tale of power and belonging. Ancient rulers governed in their own languages, which grew stronger at the expense of others already being spoken in their kingdoms. As a result, many smaller-scale languages, such as Welsh, Breton and Catalan, started to be marginalized, and some went into decline. Countries across nineteenth-century Europe began copying the monolingual framework, and schooling their young citizens in their 'state' language. It wasn't long before people started talking about 'foreign languages' (*langues étrangères*, *idiomas extranjeros*, *Fremdsprachen*). This cultural 'othering' of languages and their speakers had – and continues to have – a significant impact on society.

Some good news

This may come as a surprise, but no one is *strictly* monolingual. Even if you think you speak only one language, or if you insist that you don't have 'a gift for languages', you're absorbing snippets from other tongues all the time. We all incorporate new terms from different vernaculars into our vocabularies, and influences from different cultures frequently have an impact on us as we go through life. Some examples are *siesta*, *origami*, *wok*, *yoga*, *paparazzi* and *muesli*. These widely understood words have been adopted from Spanish, Japanese, Chinese, Hindi, Italian and Swiss-German, respectively.

In fact, around 80% of the entries in any dictionary of the English language are borrowed from other languages!

If you're a coffee lover, you may have bought a *latte* in the past. Perhaps you paired it with a *pain au chocolat*. If you're familiar with both items, you already know the Italian for 'milk' (*latte*) and the French for 'bread' (*pain*). Like so many other words, these have been imported through commerce into various languages. They've become so much a part of Western culture that they don't need translating anymore.

In addition to absorbing such terms, it's likely that even the least-experienced traveller has the ability to conjure up useful snippets from different languages to form a passable sentence. If you were in a Lisbon train station and asked someone 'Quelle hora next treno pour Madrid?', it's likely that you would be understood by speakers of Portuguese.

Most people end up employing bits of other languages in basic communication without attempting to become fluent in any of them. Over the course of a lifetime, this can amount to quite a language repertoire for international use. As humans, we're also prone to supplement what we're trying to say with hand gestures and facial expressions: these are additional tools we can use to cover any gaps in communication.

Minding the gap

You may have heard that some people are reluctant to learn another language because they're embarrassed or afraid to make mistakes. But what if you had no choice? What follows is a fictional scenario that will hopefully make an important point.

The day you had to use another language

Picture yourself cycling through the Balkans, on your way to take up a gap-year post teaching English in Athens. You'd hoped to learn some Greek after your A level results came out, but there were a lot of goodbyes to get through once school was finished, and then you managed to blag some tickets to Glastonbury. Somewhere along the way, studying Greek lost its attraction.

So far on your trip, you've been using Google Translate to order food and book accommodation, first from speakers of German in Austria and then from speakers of Slavic languages on your ride down the Adriatic coast. But you now find yourself stranded in a tiny Greek harbourside village. You'd been planning to catch the ferry, but your bike got a puncture and you missed the day's last crossing. You're hungry, you're tired and your smartphone's dead. There are a few public signs (καπηλειό, δημόσια, τουαλέτα, Εκκλησία), but they don't make any sense to you, and no smartphone means no Google Translate!

You follow the sound of some voices coming from inside a small, whitewashed building. It turns out to be the local taverna (so that's what καπηλειό meant). The owner welcomes you warmly and you smile back at his friendly face, but you don't understand a word he's saying. To make matters trickier, neither he nor any of the fishermen drinking *ouzo* at the bar can understand you. This is a real challenge!

Still, alerted by your stressed state, the locals recognize that you're a stranger in need. They soon gather some clues about your situation, as you use body language to convey meaning: you point towards the deflated tyre; you rub your empty stomach; you mime sleep. They help you with your puncture and offer you some dried fish and some wine. You're finally able to relax, sinking contentedly into a makeshift bed upstairs. Your thank you signs are easily understood when morning comes.

You've discovered that, despite neglecting your Greek studies, you already shared a language with your temporary hosts. They understood your gestures, so they offered you kindness and support. But what if you'd wanted to talk to the fishermen about the 2008 global financial crisis or, perhaps a more likely possibility, enquire about which local fish were best to eat? How well would you have fared then?

While facial expressions and hand gestures are great for covering gaps in communication, they can get you only so far. You miss out on so much without words. In some ways, your experience is akin to that of April at the start of this chapter, who lives side by side with people she cannot communicate with in their mother tongue. April's use of English is a bit like your use of body language in our scenario. To really understand her Hispanic American neighbours, April needs to learn Spanish. To really understand your rescuers, the fishermen, you need to learn Greek!

How did our ancestors communicate?

Humans have always been resourceful when it comes to finding ways to communicate down the passage of time or with speakers of other languages. Way back, people left drawings on rocks to record the things they did. The prehistoric representation in Figure 4 – made by blowing pigments over hands held against a cave wall – says to others: we were here.

Soon, our early ancestors started to use elementary tools – sticks, pebbles and beads – for counting and adding up. In due course, the means deployed to convey wordless information diversified. Hawaiians knotted strings and Mesopotamians scratched marks into wet pats of clay for record keeping. The Incas and other early civilizations wove intricate textiles to demonstrate social status.

One such decorative technique is called ikat, which is a central element of Austronesian culture. It functioned in the same way as a language: passing on values and norms, instilling a sense of belonging in the community, and signalling owners' social classes. Materials woven using ikat were saved as heirlooms; used in births, marriages and deaths; and involved in the formation of political alliances.

Figure 4 Cueva de los manos, Argentina. (By Christof Berger. This file is licensed under the Creative Commons Attribution-Share Alike 3.0 Unported license.)

To dispatch information across long distances, both visual and acoustic means of communication were used. For instance, smoke signals, being simple in both design and execution, were widely deployed in ancient civilizations. The Chinese are known to have employed them to relay messages along the Great Wall. Another example is the evolution – in places as far apart as Alaska, Africa and Oceania – of various kinds of whistled 'speech'. This was used to send news, to warn of danger or to gather people together. In parts of the Canary Islands, for example, the Gomeran whistle (*Silbo Gomero*) was an effective way of communicating across the region's deep ravines and narrow valleys; the technique is still taught in schools there today.

All of these languages – be they knotted, woven, smoke-propelled or whistled – came into being to facilitate local communication between different groups of people: an early form of multilingualism. Later, numerous artefacts left behind by early civilizations (coins, etchings, stone and pottery), far away from their own homelands, showed that cross-language practice was becoming more widespread.

People then realized that they'd get more done if they started to pick up words from speakers of other tongues. Many ended up using snippets of different languages out of necessity or when exchanging goods and knowledge. We know that having skills in languages has been considered useful and good for business since ancient times. Three millennia ago, for example, King Hammurabi of Babylon (in present-day Iraq) exploited his thriving city's growing cultural mix for a range of practical purposes. He employed bilingual citizens as translators and rewarded foreign traders who acted as cross-cultural brokers. With their diverse language skills, they played a key role in facilitating long-range trade with distant markets and in gathering intelligence about resources, new technologies and enemies.

As trade expanded and wealth increased, people started to develop an appetite for ever more diverse goods. They wanted luxury textiles, tasty spices, precious materials and more. Travelling entrepreneurs therefore set out to obtain silk from China; cinnamon, ginger and pepper from India; and amber from the Baltic. A multi-lingual community of dealers ended up bartering for commodities on trade routes, both over land and by sea. The map below shows the extensive maritime and continental trade network that had evolved by 200 C.E. Stretching from the Mediterranean to China, this became known as the Silk Road. (This ancient Silk Road concept has now been revived as China's Belt and Road Initiative, for planned cooperation between Eurasian countries.)

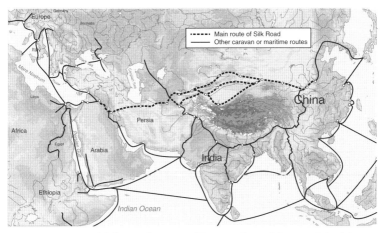

Figure 5 Map of Silk Road routes. (Figure adapted from original image found on Wikimedia Commons.)

Among the many ancient travellers who followed this route were the Chinese, Persians, Somalis, Greeks, Syrians, Romans, Armenians and Indians. In their endeavour to exchange information and peddle their products, these peoples started to develop and use trade languages when they didn't have a language or dialect in common. These were either languages with many speakers or were mixed jargons, akin to the pidgins that evolved later on, in colonial times.[17]

Knowing other people's languages has brought opportunities and prosperity to many individuals through the ages, and Marco Polo, who travelled from his native Venice to China twice (in 1266 and again a decade later), is a prime example. In his travelogue *The Marvels of the World* (published in 1300), he famously wrote that he knew several languages (Turkic, Persian and possibly Arabic and Mongolian, in addition to some less widely spoken local languages) that he used to connect with buyers and sellers from many cultures on his journeys as a merchant.

People have also deployed their knowledge of languages to engage in activities on the other side of the law: pirates, thieves and spies were of a practical bent and used terms from different vernaculars to further their illicit trade.

By being open to learning new ways of communicating, individuals from all walks of life were able to build a rapport with others, making it easier to negotiate the prices of goods – or to trick passers-by.

We know that in Medieval times, traders and the nobility could speak a number of languages. So, like Marco Polo, the Holy Roman Emperor Charles V (who reigned over much of Western Europe in the sixteenth century) could operate in various vernaculars. The story goes that:

> *If it was necessary to talk with God, he would talk in Spanish (which language suggests itself for the graveness and majesty of the Spaniard); if with friends, in Italian (for the dialect of the Italians was one of familiarity); if to caress someone, in French (for no language is tenderer than theirs); if to threaten someone or to speak harshly to them, in German (for their entire language is threatening, rough and vehement).*

For this enigmatic ruler, languages weren't just for practical use: they also had an emotional role (even if we might not agree with his characterizations). Today, this affective dimension of language is widely exploited in marketing strategies. The approach that's used seeks to invoke positive feelings in consumers, and match those feelings with the particular products or services on offer.[18]

Back to Greece

Let's return to the scenario we introduced earlier. While you may have assumed that knowing English was enough to get by in Greece, this wasn't the case, as you soon found out when you sought help in that harbourside tavern. Now we're going to see how well you get along in your teaching job.

Once in Athens, you have more success when speaking to others in English. You're teaching the subject, and neighbours seek you out with questions about ways of saying things. But you still find yourself relying on your smartphone for translations every time you buy food in a street market, need spare parts for your bike or speak to your landlady. This is time consuming and frustrating for everyone. So you start to pepper your speech with bits and pieces of Greek that you've picked up here and there. You notice this gradually getting you more attention. Sometimes it even feels like the people are adopting you as one of theirs. You're beginning to understand one of the fundamental truths of communication: you fare better when you try to reach the hearts of those around you. And in fact, you'd already touched on the emotional side of communicating with someone from another culture without realizing it: when you substituted your English words with gestures to speak with your host and the fishermen on that exhausted evening in the taverna.

So what's the lesson here? It is that people normally require a reason to learn and use another language. Our ancestors were resourceful in their interactions with strangers when on the move, buying or selling, allowing them to reap economic and social rewards. What we need to understand from history is that the human brain isn't naturally monolingual: it's perfectly suited to working in multiple languages, and doing so confers an evolutionary advantage on our species, at any age.

This conclusion is backed up by work in developmental psychology, where it has been shown that infants can detect language differences from a young age. One study demonstrated that babies who were exposed to videos of people speaking English and French discriminated between the different stimuli they heard and saw (reading lip movements).[19] This suggests that humans are multilingual-ready in infancy. So, turning this around: are those who speak only one language failing to reach their full potential?

In the next section, we'll see that speaking more than one language is not only commonplace in many parts of the world: it's essential.

The multilingual 'normal'

You may know people who can speak a language other than yours. These friends of yours might be bilingual thanks to their family life, or they might have learned a second language at school and are always looking to practise their French or Spanish (which is how you found out).

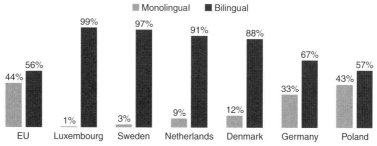

Figure 6   Percentage of bilingual speakers in the EU. (*Source*: *Europeans and Their Languages, 2006*. Special Eurobarometer 243, European Commission. Figure created by John Hogan.)

In continental Europe you'll frequently come across individuals who know multiple languages (see Figure 6),[20] but it's not so common in Britain. This is partly because of its geographic location and perhaps also due to the fact that many native English speakers don't feel the need to learn another language because theirs is so widely used. But as we shall see below, numerous people around the globe don't know any English, or only know a little, so becoming bilingual will open doors that may remain closed if you choose to remain monolingual.

But which doors, you might ask? And where? Let's take a brief journey through our world's multilingual landscape to find out.

Multilingualism in countries

Many regions, all over the world, are densely multilingual (see Figure 7). What does this mean for people?

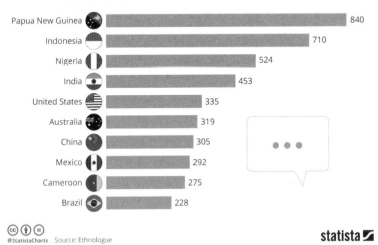

The Countries With The Most Spoken Languages
Number of living languages spoken per country in 2019

Papua New Guinea	840
Indonesia	710
Nigeria	524
India	453
United States	335
Australia	319
China	305
Mexico	292
Cameroon	275
Brazil	228

@StatistaCharts   Source: Ethnologue

statista

Figure 7   The countries with the most spoken languages. (*Source*: Statista. Available at www.statista.com/chart/3862/the-countries-with-the-most-spoken-languages/.)

In Africa for example, many are often at least trilingual. They'll generally know one European language (French, English, Portuguese, Spanish or Italian: these are often taught because of historical imperial presence in a country), sometimes they might have some Arabic (particularly in North Africa), and often they'll know at least one or two local or regional languages. In India, some knowledge of English (in addition to Hindi) is traditionally widespread and complements interactions in local and regional languages. And like their ancestors, many speakers in a variety of places around the world use several languages every day to buy, sell or find their way. They often won't be able to speak each of their languages equally well, but they'll have learned how to get by. For them, switching between languages is normal: quite unremarkable.

Several countries around the globe formally recognize more than one language, too. Singapore has four official languages, for example; South Africa has 11, India 23 and Bolivia 37 (the most of any country worldwide). These nations have systems in place for official communication, in public administration and in education, to ensure that no one is left behind and that day-to-day tasks run smoothly for all. Some countries prioritize the use of selected languages in public dealings. For instance, Bolivia gives primacy to Spanish, India to both English and Hindi, and South Africa often chooses English for state discourse.

In Europe, Belgium and Luxembourg are both formally trilingual: the former with French, German and Flemish; the latter with German, French and Luxembourgish. Switzerland operates in four languages, as you'll readily notice when travelling across the country. Leaving Genève (Geneva) in the west by train, you'll hear announcements being made in French first. Then, as you ride through the Swiss midlands, passing through Bern and Zürich, they'll be in German first. Once you've crossed the Alps and reached the Engadin region in the southeast, they'll be in the (lesser-used) Romansh language first. And finally, as you arrive in Lugano, you'll be greeted in Italian. As a passenger, you'll be served by the conductor or caterer in any of these national languages (but less so in Romansh), alongside English.

The EU has 24 official languages, and more than 60 regional and minority languages are spoken across its territories. Most EU citizens are given the opportunity to learn multiple languages, acquiring them at school and, as we shall see in Chapter 7, in further and higher education. The specific language choices made in each country vary, but schools will typically offer one neighbouring language (German in Denmark, for example) as well as a more widespread one (often English or Spanish). In Britain, a sustained approach to language teaching is largely absent from the school curriculum. Whatever the reasons for this position having been adopted by former UK governments and maintained by the present one, this can present a barrier to UK graduates when it comes to cross-language interactions overseas, as we'll see in Chapter 5.

In practice, all countries are multilingual, of course. What I mean by this is that no matter what language policy a country's schools adopt or how many official languages the country has, many of its citizens will speak in a range of different tongues. Moreover, recent EU expansion has meant that more people can cross national borders easily for work, leisure or study (although fresh restrictions have been brought in during the Covid-19 pandemic). The last few years have also seen a big increase in the number of international refugees, and everyone who is on the move takes their own language, or languages, with them. The increases in social mixing mean that linguistic and cultural diversity are a more visible everyday reality in most places. Naturally, hosting people from all over the world means providing them with education, health care, housing and access to information. This brings challenges, but also opportunities, as we shall see in Chapter 5.

Multilingualism in cities

With all this social mobility, you don't have to go abroad to hear different languages being spoken. Particularly if you live in a town or city, you'll already be aware of the multilanguage soundscape around you. Large metropolitan cities are magnets for people from across the globe, and as such they contain complex language dynamics. For example, around a third of Londoners today (about 2.5 million people) were born overseas. This results in the city having incredibly diverse neighbourhoods that are home to more than 300 language communities. If you live in London, then, multilingualism is on your doorstep.

A recent article in *The Guardian* showcased the work of the supergeographer Oliver O'Brien from University College London. It described how Oliver heard numerous languages jockeying for position in his head as he walked around London. The picture was the same below ground too, as he descended into the Tube network. Oliver decided to combine statistical data from the UK Census with the familiar lines of the city's underground network to create a series of 'Tube Tongue' maps of several languages that are widely spoken by people using the underground stations (see Figure 8).[21]

Some common languages in the city's boroughs other than those represented on the map opposite are Turkish, Somali, Tamil and Farsi. The list goes on. In some areas, street signage reflects this variety, particularly above shops that cater for the diverse clientele. In inner London, where work life and social life are closely associated, it's normal for speakers of scores of different languages to mingle. This is an example of *metrolingualism*, a term coined by linguists Alastair Pennycook and Emi Otsuji. It's an everyday expression for a cosmopolitan outlook, and it can be found in every metropolitan city around the world.

Cross-language communication often works well, but sometimes it can prove difficult, particularly in public places. In such a setting, surely English is the solution to communication problems? Not always. While it's the most widely spoken language in the UK, more than 4 million residents say they don't use English as their primary language.[22] What is more, a proportion of these people (mainly small children, the elderly, some women and the infirm) find it hard to develop any mastery of the language (we'll discuss the work of public service interpreters to bridge language gaps in Chapter 5).

In contrast, many of the individuals who arrive in the UK from around the world do speak English. Yet some also choose to maintain their primary language and pass it on to their children.

Figure 8 Representation of central London's most-spoken second languages, mapped by Tube stop. Some example stations are labelled with the language most used there, and the different shadings, from lightest (white) to darkest (black), represent Indian languages (Bengali, Gujarati, Punjabi, Urdu), Japanese, Tagalog, Chinese languages (Cantonese, Mandarin and Hokkien), Arabic, Polish, Italian, Spanish, Portuguese and French. (Figure courtesy of Oliver O'Brien, Consumer Data Research Centre 2020, based on Crown Copyright data.)

The bilingual abilities of these people constitute a vast language resource that can be used to benefit both their communities and the country as a whole. The languages that many of them speak will often complement those that are commonly learned in the Western world, so they represent an asset (as King Hammurabi already knew all those years ago). Numerous grassroots initiatives have emerged that harness this vast pool of language abilities. Many cities across Europe now participate in EU-wide schemes (e.g. EUROCITIES and LUCIDE) that produce toolkits for shared social practice.[23]

Multilingualism around the world
Consider the following facts.

▶ We live in a world in which around 7,000 languages are (currently) spoken.
▶ Of those 7,000 languages, 2,500 are considered to be endangered.
▶ More than half the world's population speaks just 23 dominant languages.

Why do we have so many languages? Why do they have such contrasting fates? Why are so many languages at risk? Why are some of the world's languages so influential?

Numerous attempts have been made to explain why humans ended up with so many languages. One story about this diversity is in the Old Testament of the Bible. This interprets the worldwide multiplicity of languages as a result of God punishing humans' hubris for trying to build a tower (in Babel) to reach the heavens. A more likely explanation is that language ecologies gradually evolved, merged and shifted as populations sought out new regions where they could settle. Like the peoples who spoke them, some languages grew while others decreased. Some, of course, died out.

As mentioned above, around a third of the world's 7,000 or so languages are now considered to be endangered (like countless biological species around the globe). But populations are more stable now than they were in the time of our foraging ancestors, so what's happening? Numerous social, environmental and economic pressures are at work here. In Indonesia, Australia and the Pacific, floods, earthquakes and volcanic eruptions have displaced many people. In the Tropics, in parts of Africa and in the Amazon, international companies have moved in to grow monocultures, thereby destroying the natural habitats of indigenous populations. In parts of the Himalayas, major dam projects are underway that submerge the livelihoods of communities. As a result, tens of thousands of people, often from fragile language ecologies, are having to leave their homelands to survive.

Many of those on the move will be expected to adapt to more dominant languages, such as English, Chinese, Hindi, Spanish or Arabic. Some of these migrants will continue to live at the margins, speaking their own languages, which may well die with them. Others, particularly younger generations, will adopt the languages of their host societies, seizing their economic opportunities and prospering, but their own languages may as a result become diluted over time, and eventually disappear. Either way, with fewer speakers, many minority languages are struggling to survive. As more and more people switch their primary languages to global ones, scores more of these less used languages have come under threat. Survival International has forecast that about 50% of the world's languages are set to disappear by the year 2050.[24] One of the at-risk languages is from the UK: Scots Gaelic. It could become extinct within a decade, according to current estimates.[25] In fact, as per UNESCO's *Atlas of the World's Languages in Danger*,[26] a language dies somewhere on our planet every two weeks.

Still, in an age of growing migration, knowing another language is crucial for those on the move, as it increases their chances of rebuilding their lives away from their homelands. The limitations caused by speaking just one language leave many vulnerable, exposed and trapped in poverty.

The case for languages

Let's return to our story about you. In Greece, you may never progress beyond using a smattering of everyday Greek. What's more, you may well end up forgetting much of what you learned once you get back home. You may come to see yourself as someone who was never even remotely bilingual. And yet new neural connections will have been formed in your brain, enriching the memories of your gap year – and, perhaps, increasing the intensity with which you tell stories about it in the years to come. You will have developed an awareness of the real benefits that come with using another language. Education is what remains after you've forgotten everything you learned in school, as Albert Einstein supposedly remarked.

Your experience will have brought you some other insights too. Many people think that everyone has at least a little knowledge of English. And it's true that English is the language that numerous speakers will turn to when they don't share a first language. After all, it's all around us in many places nowadays, driven by the language's ubiquity in science, in technology and in the flow of the global economy. So perhaps someone who's grown up in the UK – with its long-standing links to the Commonwealth and the US – will find it hard to believe that, in fact, 80% of the world's population doesn't know English.

What's more, the global economy may well be moving away from the English-speaking powerhouses. Indeed, there's some talk of the world being at the start of an 'Asian Century'. Economists predict that China's growth will soar during our lifetimes, alongside the economies of Brazil, India, Russia, Mexico and South Korea, among others. As a result, people in many parts of the world might be better off learning the languages of these growth markets: perhaps Portuguese, Russian, Hindi or Mandarin Chinese. This change is already underway in the UK: we've seen a drop in the take-up of German and French at GCSE level and a surge in students opting for other languages, especially Spanish and Mandarin Chinese.

Choosing a language

Once you've decided to learn another language, which one should you pick? For many, English is a popular choice. After all, it is prominent across the globe: in commerce, in films, in popular music, and, of course, across the internet. But what if English is your mother tongue? Here are some thoughts on other languages:

▶ Mandarin Chinese is an attractive option, not least because of China's expected growth in the coming years and decades. This tonal language is culturally distant from Western ones, though, and its traditional script can be difficult to master.

▶ Spanish is currently quite a popular language choice in the UK, thanks to its wide usage in Central and South America.

▶ Portuguese (in a variant that's slightly different to that spoken in Europe) is the main language of Brazil, a country that, like China, is showing signs of accelerating economic growth.

▶ Arabic doesn't seem to have sparked the interest of many British students yet, despite its rich appeal as the official language of 22 nations across the Middle East and North Africa.

▶ Italian, with its perennial links to classical Western culture and its associated pleasures, is widely studied around the world, despite the fact that it's barely spoken outside Europe.

► German is the most widely spoken primary language in Europe. It's also a *lingua franca* (that is, a language that's used by people whose native tongues are different) in parts of Central and Eastern Europe.

► French is the second most widespread primary language in Europe, and it has native speakers on many continents, including Africa and the Americas.

Many of these languages are used for the purposes of wider communication by a variety of international organizations, and all bar German and Portuguese are official languages of the United Nations. The British Council has predicted – on cultural, economic and educational grounds – that these languages (along with Turkish) will be the languages of the future. These are often people's first choice, so you should be able to find several of them among the study options available to you.

Changing language needs

What insights can we gain from this whistle-stop tour of the world's language landscape?

A rich diversity of languages is our social reality. Throughout history, a knowledge of languages has consistently been one of the most vital and efficient tools we have to help us bond, build, unite, learn and make things happen. Multilingualism is part of what characterizes us as humans. Language contacts have always been made, and then intensified through migration and exploration, travel and trade, conquest and displacement. Learning a new tongue is not a modern phenomenon, and our brains are perfectly suited to the task, at any age. Languages have come and gone over the centuries, with the more widely used ones having always attracted students eager to be able to converse with more people, in more places (in ancient times it was Old Persian, Greek and Latin, for example).

Today, propelled by communication technology, English appears to occupy centre stage. It's widely used, for sure, but it's no *passe-partout*. It isn't a master key to the doors of every culture, as your imagined Greek experience above made clear. It has for company other languages that have spread as different countries go through periods of rapid economic development. As the global economy diversifies, multilinguals are becoming necessary in more diverse, and more complex, situations. For this reason, your language trajectory may well take some unexpected turns. (In Chapter 4, you'll encounter several individuals whose language studies gave them new directions in life.)

This chapter has sought to raise your awareness of the way people's language needs have changed throughout history. In our journey through time and space, we've seen that languages have always mattered to humans. The communication challenges we face today aren't unique or new. What *is* new are the tools we have to overcome them and the choices we can make – and, perhaps, people's views on languages.

It's now high time I tried to help you with your decision-making. In the next chapter I'll bust some of the myths you may have heard about language learning and bilingualism, and I'll acquaint you with the facts.

CHAPTER 3

Are languages for me?

WE HAVE ALREADY DISCUSSED SOME of the reasons you might want to learn a language. Perhaps you're keen on travelling, in which case a knowledge of how the locals speak in your chosen destination will clearly be beneficial. Or maybe you fancy volunteering in one of Italy's migrant 'boot camps' during your gap year. Would your interest in marine biology be cemented by signing up for a reef surveying project in Madagascar? Surely an internship in Germany would benefit your mechanical engineering studies? In all these cases, learning the locally used language (Italian, French or German) will help you to understand your subject and surroundings better.

Languages can make things happen

Languages are essential to who we are, and they help us relate to the world around us. With an additional language, you can let your natural curiosity take you in new directions: aid work, for example. You might end up in Bergamo, helping refugees deal with their trauma via language work. Or maybe you'll find yourself attending a local conservation event in Antananarivo (Madagascar's capital), learning about the threat posed to whale sharks by the overfishing of reef fish. In Frankfurt, perhaps you'll stumble across an engineering trade show and discover why 'Made in Germany' holds such a cachet in that industry.

Being able to navigate your new surroundings with the perspective of the locally used language shows your respect for your hosts. You'll find that people open up to you when you talk to them on their own terms. They may slow down to help you understand what they're talking about. They may insert small pauses into their speech so that you can confirm what's been said. They may bolster their words with gestures for clarity, or to avoid confusion. These communicative trimmings will help reduce the social barriers that strangers often have to navigate: you will be treated like a member of the club. Making a linguistic effort shows that you respect the local community, and it will change how you're perceived there.

Once you get to grips with your new language, you'll begin to feel more connected with your host society. Through your daily encounters with people, by reading posters and notices in the streets, and by attending cultural events, you'll gradually learn to appreciate your host country's way of life and the issues that move the locals. In due course, an opportunity for you to contribute to local artistic, environmental or economic endeavours may arise, helping you to form lasting connections.

There's no doubt that languages can take you places. Put simply, knowing another language enables you to communicate with more people in more situations. It means you can share stories with individuals you may otherwise never have gotten to know, and learn about their experiences. The rewards will be formative, through challenges overcome and opportunities taken up.

Language myths and facts

We've considered several benefits of studying languages, but what about the costs and the challenges? Let's look at some of the reasons people give for *not* choosing to study languages. Do any of the following remarks sound familiar to you?

- ▶ I'm no good at learning languages.
- ▶ It's difficult as well as boring: it's all about grammar rules.
- ▶ I'll never be as good as a native speaker.
- ▶ Everyone speaks English.
- ▶ I can get an instant translation from my smartphone anywhere I need it.
- ▶ I can't express what I want to say in another language.

- ▶ I don't want to travel or work abroad so I'll never use another language.
- ▶ I don't want to go into a job such as language teaching or translating, so what's the point?
- ▶ I don't know which language to choose: are some more useful than others?
- ▶ I'm afraid of a challenge: which languages are easier/harder to learn?
- ▶ I can't fit it into my schedule: there are more important subjects!
- ▶ Language learning has gone out of fashion.
- ▶ Language degrees are taught in English.
- ▶ My parents had poor experiences when learning a language.

Opinions of this sort abound, but is it really the case, to take just one example, that someone who relies on their smartphone to undertake translation has an advantage over someone who has the necessary vocabulary in their head? It's easy to get caught up in misconceptions about language learning, and if those miconceptions are reinforced in public, by the media and by politicians, such views risk stifling potential learners' dispositions towards languages.

Fake views

I will address each of the views listed above one by one before this chapter is done. We will puncture some of the myths and dispel the stereotypes that persist about language learning.

'I'm no good at learning languages.' Given an opportunity to do so, most of us are capable of learning another language. In fact, by reading this text, you have proven that you're comfortable with at least one! If you understand the mechanics of one language, you're fit to delve into another, whatever your age. You don't require a special gene or talent: all you need is interest and perseverance. A natural inclination is obviously beneficial when learning any new skill. With sport, working out your physical muscles leads to progression and satisfaction; in the case of languages, it's your mental muscles that need to be attended to (there is more on this below).

As you saw in the previous chapter, the world around us is multilingual: knowing several languages is commonplace for many humans, and having that ability gives them the potential to achieve more. The same applies to any monolingual speaker, provided they have an incentive. When you say you're no good at learning languages, what you might inadvertently be implying is that most of the world is more capable than you are: that can't possibly be true!

'It's difficult as well as boring: it's all about grammar rules.' Naturally, acquiring the basics of a new skill requires time and effort. But there's much more to learning a language than exercise and practice: it can be fun too! There are many freely available apps to help you get started, Duolingo being a widely known example. These can make the initial phase of mastering a language more entertaining and they can enrich your learning experience. You'll also be offered plenty of opportunities for interaction in more formal settings.

Remember, languages are social organisms: they are living and growing, and they aren't by nature made up of strict rules. What is more, as we'll see in Chapter 4, learning a language can unlock a person's creativity and is similar in its energizing effects to painting or drawing. This has major consequences for personal growth and national economic development, which many insightful business leaders (your potential future employers!) are keen to exploit.

'I'll never be as good as a native speaker.' No one expects you to sound like someone who's been raised in the language you're learning. In fact, aiming for 'native speaker' command isn't a reliable yardstick and can mean different things to different people: having no accent, equal fluency, making no mistakes. Yet even in our primary language we can find ourselves stuck for words at times, or struggling to find the best way of saying something. We're all capable of committing errors, too. Here are two examples in English. Can you spot the grammatical errors?

▶ None of my neighbours are able to speak Mandarin Chinese.
▶ If I was rich, I would buy a big car.

Pause for a moment. You understand both sentences. Both are clear in terms of meaning, even if you'd temporarily forgotten that 'none' is singular and if you *were* unaware of the uses of the subjunctive. Learning another language will make you more language-aware and improve your ability to detect how languages work.

What really matters in a language-diverse setting is that you can *function* in different languages (at whatever level of proficiency) and that you feel at ease when switching between them. As we shall see in Chapter 7, language ability can be measured by progression in two active parts (speaking and writing) and two passive parts (listening and reading). These skills are assessed at a proficiency level that's appropriate for you: beginner, intermediate or advanced.

'Everyone speaks English.' There is perhaps an intuitive belief in certain parts of the world that everyone speaks English. And it's true that the language is used widely in science, medicine, business and entertainment, and it dominates the internet, exerting a huge influence on learners' language choices today. But statistics show that you'd be wrong to think that knowing English is enough to allow you to communicate with everyone. As we saw in the previous chapter, just 20% of the world's population have any significant knowledge of English: that means that four in five people don't!

And only 1 in 20 people use English as their primary language, with the remainder having various degrees of proficiency, so many will struggle to engage in a conversation in English.

'**I can get an instant translation from my smartphone anywhere I need it.**' Translation technology does have considerable potential in offering assistance to users of different languages in situations of incomprehension. You may well be able to book a hotel room in Cantonese using Google Translate. But Google as a translation tool is not omniscient. In its current version, it's not fit for the purpose of conveying the everyday nuances and deeper meanings of human interaction. Moreover, while Google, Facebook, Twitter and their ilk cover a growing range of languages, by no means all are covered. Instead of focusing on how the culture of using technology can *replace* human language learning, we need to look at how the former can *enhance* the latter.

'**I can't express what I want to say in another language.**' It's only natural for beginners to sense a barrier as they attempt to glue together the pieces of their nascent language skills. This is because learners tend to look *at* a new language as if it were a finished product. But with practice, they'll soon begin to look *through* it: that is, to treat their learning as an ongoing process. Besides, when talking, we engage our entire selves: our bodies serve as additional, silent means of communication. As your imagined experience in Greece showed, we also draw on facial expressions, tones of voice, body movements and gestures as cues to help us make sense of what's being said. These key partners to speech convey emotions regardless of a speaker's (or listener's) language.

'**I don't want to travel or work abroad, so I'll never use another language.**' You already know that you don't have to go abroad to hear other languages: with increasing mobility, society has rapidly become more language diverse. According to the 2011 Census, more than 350 languages are spoken in the UK, and we've already discussed London's sizeable and language-rich communities. This heterogeneity of speakers right on our doorsteps presents a range of social and economic opportunities for bilinguals, in both the public and private sectors as well as in everyday life. Languages could therefore very well come into play in your life too. You might find a job in a British-Canadian company, for example, where some knowledge of French would be an advantage. Or maybe you'll fall in love with your new Spanish-speaking neighbour.

Some facts

Just as with language learning, there are also many myths about bilingualism, as touched on above. Here too, the facts often tell another story. We'll now review some emerging evidence about the cognitive and emotional gains that accrue to bilinguals. The good news is that knowing more than one language – whether it's your grandparents' Welsh or your school Spanish – has been found to improve your intelligence.

Research suggests that, all else being equal, bilingual children tend to display enhanced overall ability compared with their monolingual peers, performing better across the school curriculum. Why is this? It turns out that the bilingual brain is structurally more elaborate[27] and more pliable[28] than that of its monolingual counterpart. What is more, brain scans show that the former is 'denser' than the latter, and that it becomes denser still as language proficiency increases. This is especially the case in the brain's left hemisphere, where many communication and language skill centres are located.

Of course, such benefits don't come without effort. Bilinguals may well end up with more grey matter than monolinguals[29] but they have to work at it. It all depends on how long you've been oper-ating in more than one language, how often you use your languages, and how frequently you switch between them.[30] The brain, then, is like a cognitive muscle: it gets stronger, bigger and more flexible the more it's used. So, if you've got two or more languages constantly competing for attention, your grey matter is getting a good workout!

But how does the bilingual brain function when it's involved in processing languages? Neuroscientists have used imaging techniques to scan bilingual and monolingual brains while they are performing selected language tasks. They've found that specific brain regions are more active in bilingual production (which involves selecting one language and suppressing another). Albert Costa has produced an accessible research account of the studies he carried out in his native Catalonia, and he elaborates therein on what it means to double up on one's language capacity.[31] He sees the constant interaction of two (or more) languages in the brain as a process of 'productive conflict' that keeps an individual's languages cognitively exercised.

Some researchers have formulated what's become known as the 'bilingual advantage theory'.[32] What they propose is that the experience of managing two or more languages strengthens exec-utive control. This function is involved in such complex cognitive processes as attention and inhibition (focusing on a specific task while ignoring irrelevant information). Among additional suggested cognitive gains are enhanced working memory, greater mental flex-ibility, better problem-solving skills, and cognitive reserve in later years. Honing these essential skills would therefore seem to serve as a lifelong asset, in your studies, future employment and beyond (more on this is in Chapter 7).

Let's look at a work-related example, which comes from obser-vations of London taxi drivers (known colloquially as 'cabbies'). As Jabr Ferris reports in *Scientific American*,[33] cabbies-in-training spend three to four years riding around the city on mopeds learning the streets in order to earn their licences. They then have to pass a battery of memory tests to earn what's called 'The Knowledge'. Their intensive training involves memorizing around 25,000 city streets. In addition, drivers must be able to calculate the swiftest route between any two points in their network while navigating their way through a maze of possibilities. Ferris refers to research that shows that, as a result of their training, cabbies end up having larger-than-average memory centres in their brains.[34] This probably occurs because the cabbies' ongoing mental efforts cause physical changes and an increase in the size of a part of the brain called the hippocampus. Its growth is thought to happen because new neurons located in that region of the brain form denser connections with one another.

These findings suggest that learning (whether it's languages or, in this case, street names) is a powerful motor that keeps our grey matter healthy and actively engaged. What is more, the cognitive benefits appear to have an impact on an individual's social interactions. Bilinguals have been found to display enhanced cultural sensitivity, empathy and tolerance towards others.[35] This could well be because they are able to block out their own language when switching to that of their interlocutor, meaning they can concentrate more on the feelings and beliefs of others. Languages, then, appear to influence both our thoughts and our behaviour. They are truly a gateway to cultural understanding.

Lingering reservations?

It may be that you've found this news about the transformative, brain-enhancing qualities of being bilingual a bit of a surprise. Many people don't bargain for these extra benefits when they start thinking about learning another language! That doesn't mean you won't have any lingering concerns, though, so let's finish going through our list from earlier.

'I don't want to go into a job such as language teaching or translating, so what's the point?' You certainly don't have to! There are numerous ways in which you can capitalize on your language knowledge. Languages play a central role in *all* facets of life, so they're an asset in many occupations and leisure activities (as we shall see in subsequent chapters). Besides, learning another language (whether or not it's still in use today) helps you gain greater knowledge about the mechanics of language itself. This awareness can carry over to your primary language and make you a better communicator, which will help you greatly in your studies at school and university.

'I don't know which language to choose: are some languages more useful than others?' Certain languages do enjoy higher 'brand recognition' than others. Many students today make language choices by assessing their perceived utility. For instance, studying Spanish, Mandarin Chinese, Arabic or Russian might appeal based on their anticipated 'return on investment': these languages are associated with a wide speaker base and, therefore, their potential to lead to material gain. However, it's impossible to predict which languages will be of global importance in the future, or where the next opportunity or obstacle might arise. All languages, big or small, alive or dead, add value to our lives, offering social as well as economic benefits.

'I'm afraid of a challenge: which languages are easier/harder to learn?' There is no simple way of determining whether a language is hard or easy to learn. This is partly because the difficulty of learning a language can be assessed in a variety of ways: we need to look at everything from pronunciation to grammar to script. For example, Mandarin Chinese, while relatively simple grammatically, is complex when it comes to mastering tonality and *hanzi*, its writing system. How you perceive difficulty has more to do with your own language background and your personal goals than anything else. If you're already the proud speaker of a second language, you can likely draw on your existing language-building skills to help you tackle another (we'll discuss this in Chapters 4 and 6). And if you're studying a language because it's something you're passionate about, it's always going to be easier to learn than a subject you don't enjoy!

'I can't fit it into my schedule: there are more important subjects!' Much weight is placed in school curricula and in higher education institutions on the STEM subjects (science, technology, engineering and mathematics), often at the expense of what have recently been christened the SHAPE subjects (social sciences, humanities and the arts for people and the economy). Yet all of these disciplines are crucial components of a broad-based education that will equip students with vital, complementary skills in the twenty-first century. Languages form an important part of this well-rounded skill set and, as we've seen above, contribute to better overall performance.

Some institutions, both schools and universities, offer selected subjects through the medium of a 'target language'. So, as a speaker of English, you might be able to learn physics in French, or geography in Spanish. This approach is called Content and Language Integrated Learning (CLIL). Another option for cementing your proficiency in a new language is to spend an immersive period in a region where that language is spoken, either through a student-exchange programme or as part of an internship within an organization (see Chapter 7).

'Language learning has gone out of fashion.' The demand for skilled professionals who can oscillate between different languages and cultures is growing, not diminishing. In fact, 'global competence' – that is, the ability to operate effectively in a multicultural landscape – is regarded as a fundamental skill in education. It enables learners to understand and appreciate different perspectives and engage in open and effective interactions with people from various cultural backgrounds. This initiative is based on the 2018 Programme for International Student Assessment (PISA) Global Competence Framework, which aims to empower learners to deal with the challenges of our increasingly interconnected world.[36] In many school curricula across Europe, language education plays a central role in equipping students to become active global citizens.

'Language degrees are taught in English.' It's true that some of the instruction you'll receive at university in the UK may not be delivered in your target language. However, as we'll see in Chapter 7, there will be plenty of opportunities for you to learn in the language you're studying, and you'll be encouraged to engage in extensive language practice through various online and offline resources. You will experience many different teaching methods and forms of learning, and you'll certainly utilize both English and your target language. Don't forget that part of your course may involve a study period abroad.

'My parents had poor experiences when learning a language.' Don't worry, language teaching has come a long way in the last couple of decades. Your parents may remember a time when more weight was placed on memorizing grammar rules and when less attention was paid to the ability of students to communicate effectively in another language. But the old methods have long since given way to more learner-centred contextual activities. The focus now is on building confidence and developing a range of communication skills, in settings that are relevant to students. This means a shift away from what learners *know* about a language towards what they can actually *do* with that knowledge. Students are encouraged to incorporate their personal experiences into their language-learning activities, to experiment with their target language, and to develop a *feel* for it.

Having considered these facts and fictions, I hope you'll have come away with the sense that learning a language (to any level of competence) is both practical and enriching. Building on your skill set in this way will yield educational and cognitive benefits, and you may also end up with greater compassion for others and a better global understanding. What is more, becoming bilingual is sure to open up further personal and occupational opportunities in due course. As we shall see in Chapter 5, the skills associated with learning a language are important to the economy and will continue to be so as we move towards a more global future. As you read on, you'll discover the multiple ways in which pursuing a language degree can help you make a real difference in the world.

How do I decide whether to pursue language study?

Before you embark on any course of study, you'll need to be prepared to invest time, effort and money into the venture. Since these are limited resources for all of us, you'll want to be sure about your decision. While some people are happy to follow their instincts, others look for guidance to help them make up their minds. You might be wondering about your return on investment, too.

So how do you go about making your choice?

Let's say it's your dream to learn Danish because you're fascinated by all things Goth. But if you were to study Mandarin Chinese, you'd have the opportunity to work in a family friend's software company in Shanghai when you graduate. How do you pick?

Although plumping for the latter option will probably result in direct material returns sooner, the former – while it might primarily satisfy your curiosity and yield only intangible benefits to begin with – may end up being the better choice. Imagine your surprise when your knowledge of Danish lands you a part in a Scandi Noir film, which subsequently leads to material returns you had never considered.

While this scenario might be a little far-fetched, the salient point is this: since we can't know what the future holds, we have to be prepared to take a chance sometimes. The safest bet might not always be the most rewarding one. Our ability to make decisions is ultimately what determines who we are. It's intrinsic to the human experience, and it has shaped the course taken by humankind. Our ancestors had to work out how to find resources, avoid danger and make friends, for example. And like all of us as we go through life, you will have to balance your choices against a range of possible outcomes, and your personality will shape your journey. It may be that choosing what you *want* to do, as opposed to choosing what you think you *should* do, is the best decision you ever make.

The world's ten most spoken languages are listed in Figure 9. While English is currently the most widespread additional language in terms of number of users, you can see that Chinese (and its

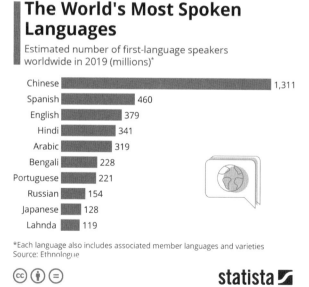

Figure 9 The world's most spoken languages. (*Source*: Statista. Available at www.statista.com/chart/12868/the-worlds-most-spoken-languages/.)

varieties, including Mandarin) tops the chart as the first (that is, native) language with the most speakers. It's the primary language of about 1.3 billion speakers (or about 16% of the world's entire population). After Chinese come Spanish, English, Hindi, Arabic (and its numerous varieties), Bengali, Portuguese, Russian, Japanese and Lahnda (which is an Indic language of the Western Punjab and adjacent areas of Pakistan).

You might see great value in learning one of the above languages, as they have many speakers, or you might consider opting for a language that's currently less prominent in the West: Malay or Turkish, say. Taking the latter route might seem more risky, but who knows? Malaysia and Turkey have potential for considerable growth in many sectors, so their languages might become more economically influential in the near future.

Which option you choose will largely depend on your risk profile. Are you risk averse? Do you thrive among the familiar and desire certainty? In that case, you might want to opt for a language (maybe German or French) the potential of which you can envisage more clearly. Or are you a risk taker? Are you driven by curiosity and maybe a certain reckless abandon? If so, a less well-known language might be right for you (although you may need a healthy dose of resilience along the way!).

How much can I expect to earn?

Naturally, the earning power of individuals with a knowledge of languages varies from one country to the next. However, several studies from around the world have shown that having an additional language (or languages) can boost income. In an article titled 'Speaking more than one language can boost economic growth', published in *World Economic Forum*,[37] Sophie Hardach refers to studies showing that workers in Florida who speak both Spanish and English earn around $7,000 (or £5,300) per year more than those who know only English. She supports her argument with findings about bilinguals from Canada, where they receive on average around 5% more than their monolingual peers. In Europe, a recent Polish study[38] points to a wage premium of around 11% for someone with an advanced command of a second language.

The benefits associated with learning specific languages are subject to the law of supply and demand. As Figure 10 shows, material advantages in Poland are currently greater for proficiency in French (22%) than they are for proficiency in German (12%), largely because the country is home to more German speakers. In the US, by contrast, German has been found to have a higher material value than French due to the relative scarcity of a skills base in the former, despite Germany's importance in trade.

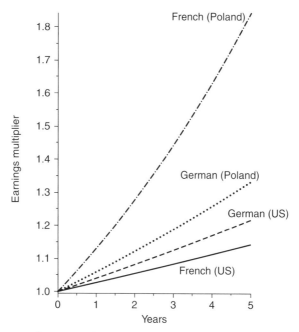

Figure 10 Salary gains from intermediate-level second-language skills.[39] (Figure created by John Hogan.)

So if you're interested in your earnings potential with regard to languages, you'll need to consider the demand for particular languages where you are or where you want to end up. For example, as a bilingual in Welsh and English, your abilities in Welsh will naturally be in greater demand in Cardiff than in Newcastle. Overall, as the latest UK government statistics (2020) show,[40] your earning capacity is considerable with languages. In fact, the median salary five years after graduation is greater for languages than for law, putting language graduates comfortably in the middle of the pack (ahead of those in biosciences, education and journalism, for example).

In brief, your decision about whether to learn another language and, if you do, which one(s) to choose will involve multiple considerations. Your choice might be guided by the language's apparent utility value, and this will factor into your cost–benefit calculations, as discussed above. Alternatively, you might be more concerned with how you want to position yourself in the world. You might feel a connection with a specific culture, perhaps through family ties. These are all valid incentives that can lead you to personal growth and to making a difference in the world.

I hope this chapter has addressed some of your concerns about studying languages, busting a few myths along the way. However, it's not possible to give you a conclusive answer as to whether a languages degree is right for you. This is the case for many reasons, not least because personal inclinations and possible options vary, and because our circumstances are constantly subject to change.

Think for a moment. What are *your* incentives? Are you driven by curiosity about other people and places, a desire to be accepted by a particular culture, the anticipated economic advantages of this course of study, your love of a particular language, or a combination of some or all of these? Whatever your eventual decision, the best advice

I can give is to trust your instincts and use your resources in a way that best satisfies your perspectives, motivations and aspirations.

We'll now move on to explore how other people have responded to diverse impetuses to learn a new language. The famous names we're going to meet in the next chapter all made the decision to master a particular language, and this became an important milestone along their road to success. I hope their stories will be a source of inspiration to you.

CHAPTER 4

What can languages do for us?

WE'VE ALREADY SEEN THE MANY rewards you can expect to gain from learning a new language. Among them are stronger communication skills, potential cognitive growth and wider opportunities in general, and all of these may, in due course, bring material benefits. Knowing languages will also open your mind and allow you to see the world in new and exciting ways. By appreciating different cultures and modes of thinking, you may come to develop greater cultural sensitivity and tolerance towards others.

As an active citizen in our rapidly changing world, cultural insight is a necessity when it comes to understanding and engaging with the key issues that affect us all every day. Since being able to communicate with one another is the best way of gaining such insight, languages clearly function as enablers or conduits. In this chapter we'll follow the life trajectories of some outstanding individuals and see how languages have enabled them to make a difference in various spheres of life.

Following your passion

People are often drawn to and value certain languages for their inherent characteristics. Think for a moment: what makes a language attractive when you hear it? The way it sounds? The culture or sense of familiarity it evokes? The person speaking it? There are those who regard learning their chosen language(s) as an ongoing love affair. This is the case for the individuals below, who come from very different walks of life. For them, following the path their adopted language led them down has been life changing. The allure of the languages they've fallen in love with comes through loud and clear in their stories.

The chef
Meet Thomasina (Tommi) Miers, founder of Mexican street-food restaurant chain Wahaca and winner of *MasterChef* (a UK television

programme) in 2005. Cooking had always been Tommi's first love. Upon graduating from Ballymaloe Cookery School in County Cork, Ireland, she travelled to Mexico. She became fascinated with the country, its food and its language. In a 2015 interview with *The Guardian*[41], Tommi discussed getting to know the language 'dish by dish' during her Mexican food odyssey. And it was not only the language that was alluring: so was the food. She was attracted to Spanish by its earthy, guttural sounds, which perfectly complemented the different flavours she encountered. Everything was all wrapped together in one package of language, food and emotion.

It is Tommi's belief, and mine, that you can't really get to grips with any culture if you're unfamiliar with its language. Food is a central part of Mexican identity. So, when you learn about the food, you are also learning about the people and their ways of doing things. But to really understand them, you have to know their language. In this way, food, culture and language are all bound together.

Tommi's personal account paints a vivid picture of how her Mexican experience and her encounters with chefs, their suppliers and clientele, all conducted in Spanish, inspired her culinary trajectory. Maybe she'd still have won *MasterChef* without knowing any Spanish, but the outstanding economic success of Wahaca (which is the phonetic spelling of the Mexican state of Oaxaca) can undoubtedly be attributed to becoming acquainted with the language. It has added value to her life both as a person and as a chef.

Our next protagonist, the writer Jhumpa Lahiri, has experienced a quite different life trajectory, but again it's one that has made her fall deeply in love with a Mediterranean language: this time Italian. We'll now follow Jhumpa on her language journey.

The writer and translator

Jhumpa, winner of the Pulitzer Prize for Fiction in 2000, has long been driven by a passion for the Italian language: so much so that she decided to move to Italy from her home in the US in 2011. There, she completely immersed herself in order to soak up the language, reading and writing only in Italian for three years.

Let's see what got her there in the first place. In an *Observer* interview with Kathryn Bromwich[42], Jhumpa talks about falling in love with Italian. She compares her experience with the language to that of a vocation. Her view is that there is nothing rational about her desire: when she speaks Italian, she feels exhilarated, stimulated and liberated.

She goes on to explain that there is 'something transgressive' about her relationship with the language. Deep down, she doesn't understand the mysterious impulse to learn Italian: it emerged out of nowhere. But she is driven by a need to acknowledge the feeling, and to follow it wherever it takes her. In Chapter 6 we'll look at the various stages of her Italian language journey.

As Jhumpa sees it, her motivation to learn Italian was *partly* driven by her ambivalent relationship with both Bengali – the language of her parents – and English, which was the language of her education and the one that became her primary language: the one in which she was published. In the same *Observer* interview she explains why she was looking for a way out of her language conflict, and how she made her escape.

When she spoke Bengali in the US, she felt alienated from her environment, with no wider connection to what was happening around her. She recalls the atmosphere in her parental home as being one of resistance, on her mother's part, to the US. Her mother had no desire to assimilate, and she continued to shape her life as if she were still in her native Calcutta. Jhumpa believes that growing up in such circumstances casused her to rebel, but in a way that meant acceptance and transformation, rather than denial and preservation.

Similarly, when she spoke English in the US, her Bengali heritage meant that she felt she did not belong there either. She therefore needed agency: to look beyond her existing language boundaries and branch out. She wanted to find her self as a person and discover her voice as a writer. Her liberation finally came about through another language: it was by entering an intimate relationship with Italian that her horizons opened up.

As we've learned from the testimonies of these two self-motivated women, language was the key that opened a door to the culture, the people and the particulars of another reality – to another way of thinking and being altogether. Tommi and Jhumpa tell us that without following their language calling, they could not have entered these new worlds. In embracing language like a passionate affair, they derived considerable personal satisfaction and ended up making names for themselves; both took risks, and both were handsomely rewarded.

From passion to utility

We'll now look at the journeys of some other individuals whose knowledge of languages has proven to be an essential tool in their chosen professions. In both the diplomatic and intelligence services, as well as in reporting, the ability to listen, talk and take action across language boundaries is paramount. Those with critical language skills, who are able to convey information in intercultural settings, have a vital role to play.

The journalist

The BBC's Security Correspondent, Frank Gardner, is known for his dedication to using languages (mainly French, German, Russian and Arabic) as a way of understanding other cultures. Frank inherited a sense of the ability of languages to open up new worlds from his diplomat parents. As he explained to Miranda Moore, while being interviewed for an article in *The Linguist*[43], his family would easily switch between French, Dutch, German and Italian at home while he was growing up. He therefore came to see languages as 'an adventure', fantasizing about them 'as a magical portal to someone else's world', much like 'the wardrobe that leads to Narnia'.

He talks with fascination about his experiences as a young student in different countries. While staying with an elderly couple on a school exchange in Germany, Frank remembers being captivated by his host's stories about fighting on the Eastern Front in World War II. Later, visiting nightclubs and riding motorbikes in France meant he came back to the UK with 'quite good conversational French' (accompanied by some very bad French slang, which, he remembers, 'appalled' his mum). But it was a trip to Morocco that eventually truly opened his eyes to a different way of life:

It was incredibly exciting. Arabic was the portal through which I was experiencing a completely different culture. Everything about it was fascinating: the way it was pronounced, the way it was written, the way people's facial expressions change when they speak Arabic.

In due course, it was his intimate knowledge of this language that enabled him to report from conflict zones across the vast Arab world. In his *Linguist* interview, Frank explains that 'languages have always been central to that journey':

It's very difficult to even get close to understanding a country if you can't speak at least a bit of its language. ... In Yemen there is no way I could have got into kidnap territory in the mountains without Arabic, negotiating which guides we were going to take, who we could trust. Even if the people you're working with, or that you're trying to interview, have got English, the fact that you have bothered to learn their language is showing them respect and they will want to help you.

Frank learned Arabic not only to enable him do his job as a reporter better, but also to help him form relationships with the people he met, often in perilous circumstances:

I hope they see me as somebody who cares about their region and is not just a visitor. I'm not just going to the Middle East because it's an assignment.

His passion for Arabic has remained strong despite being shot by Al Qaeda gunmen while working in Saudi Arabia, leaving him paralysed. This didn't curb his commitment to reporting from overseas, though, and he was subsequently awarded an OBE for his services to journalism.

Frank's knowledge of languages made him the excellent reporter he is. While languages and journalism may seem like an obvious pairing, other less predictable careers can be advanced through language study too. Even tennis!

Martina Navratilova, winner of 18 Grand Slam singles titles and one of the world's greatest ever female tennis players, is on record as saying that her multilingual abilities helped her become a star.

The sportswoman

As Martina sees it, the sport that made her name is almost like a language in its own right. She grew up playing tennis, and it became her passion. She spoke both Czech and German at home, and she learned other languages at school. Martina soon sensed that languages would help her to spread her wings. In an article in *The Independent*, she describes how her life was transformed and broadened by tennis and languages.[44] She points out that when you learn another language, you have to adapt to a new way of thinking, just as you do, stroke by stroke, in tennis.

That there is a certain logic to languages goes against the idea that you need a special gift to learn them. Just as with tennis, Martina finds that languages are straightforward to pick up but then reveal hidden complexities as you progress. For her, the organizing principle is that once you understand how a language works, you can start to make choices about how to string sets of words together.

Martina sees speaking different languages as both character forming and mind enhancing, and she believes that it has boosted her brain power (a belief backed up by lots of research about the brain, including that which we came across in the previous chapter). More specifically, her reflections support the 'bilingual advantage' theory about proposed gains strenghtening cognitive processes (working memory) as well as executive functions (attentional control), which underpin both tennis and language.

Being skilled in languages has helped Martina both on the court and off it. Her subsequent success as a sports commentator probably stems from a combination of the ease with which she speaks different languages and the precision with which she plays her sport. Martina's ability to communicate, whether with a tennis racquet or with her voice, has improved through her multilingualism.

We'll now examine the case of Matthias Maurer, who is using languages to help fulfil his ambition of becoming an astronaut.

The trainee astronaut

People with language skills play a key role in international transportation, whether by land, sea or air. The safety risks posed by misunderstandings between pilots and air traffic controllers, for example, caused by ineffective multilingual exchanges are especially severe.

They're higher still when it comes to operating a spacecraft, as Matthias Maurer, a material scientist and member of the European Space Agency (ESA) astronaut corps, explained in conversation with Miranda Moore for *The Linguist*:[45]

> *In an emergency, there needs to be a common action and if you don't understand each other you will not be effective. That's a safety issue and an absolute no-go criteria, so you must master at least enough of the language to be able to do a proper job.*

He goes on to say that it is not only in emergencies that communication is important. The overall mission objectives require the team to work efficiently together, for example, with good social dynamics. The success of any lengthy space flight and the well-being of those involved in the confines of a capsule also rely on the crew members' language skills. As Samantha Cristoforetti, another ESA trainee astronaut, points out,[46] although working closely in an international setting has its challenges, it also brings benefits in building team spirit when striving towards a common goal.

Matthias mentions watching NASA space missions on TV during his childhood in Germany but says he never seriously believed it would be him up there. When the ESA did start to recruit, he knew it was his calling. He was not successful initially, being offered only a role in crew support. But subsequent negotiations between the ESA and China's two space agencies (the Chinese National Space Administration and the Chinese Manned Space Agency) opened up new possibilities, leading him to volunteer to learn Chinese. He also learned Russian to increase his chances of serving on board the International Space Station, where all astronauts are required to speak both English and Russian. Having multiple languages at your disposal to help you understand cultural differences within an international crew is clearly important for aspiring astronauts.

From utility to creativity

Languages have considerable creative potential in the arts, and this can in turn lead to economic value. Many artists draw on languages and cultures as a source of inspiration. They are a vibrant and increasingly valued presence on the world's cultural stage. This interplay between multilingualism and creativity has been widely studied.[47] Let us now have a look at how languages can function as a catalyst for actors, singers and (would-be) linguists.

Actors

Multilingual individuals are much sought after in media and film because they are better placed to play characters in complex multicultural circumstances. The need to authentically convey experiences and emotions that aren't your own is greatly helped by a familiarity with the languages of other cultures. For one actor (Romann Berrux, who recently shot to fame in both French and English roles), performing in another language is the moment he loves most, allowing him to slip into another role that's totally different from his own personality.[48]

Several famous actors are well versed in different tongues: Jodie Foster speaks French, Italian, German and Spanish; Kristin Scott Thomas speaks French; Christoph Waltz speaks German, English and Italian; and Natalie Portman knows French, German, Spanish, Japanese and Hebrew.

And actors aren't restricted to using 'real' languages, either. Viggo Mortensen, who played Aragorn in *The Lord of the Rings* trilogy, had to learn Elvish for his famous role. Raised in Buenos Aires by a Danish father and an American mother, Viggo grew up speaking Spanish, English and Danish, adding French, Italian, Norwegian and Swedish into the mix as he got older. His flair for languages enabled him to slip into complex roles, such as World War II Captain Daru in the film *Far from Men*. In an interview in 2014 with *The Hollywood Reporter*, he explained that it's not just about getting the language right.[49] Just as he pays great attention to the clothes he wears in a movie, so he wants to also get a protagonist's accent right. To him, this means that his character (who in this case spoke French with an Algerian accent, as well as Arabic) is more believable.

Singers

In the world of music entertainment, bilingual artists enjoy a growing profile. Their ability to connect with different cultures through song gives them a huge advantage. Many Latin singers, for example, have boosted their careers with English-language or bilingual productions. One of the most famous examples is Ricky Martin (real name Enrique Martín Morales), sometimes called the King of Latin Pop. A native of Puerto Rico, Ricky began his career in the Spanish-speaking boy band Menudo. After going solo he sang only in Spanish, initially, but then also in English, moving easily between the two languages. Doing so made him a global icon.

Sofia Reyes, from Mexico, another bilingual pop idol, hit the headlines in April 2019.[50] Her 'trilingual empowerment anthem' *RIP* is a Mexican, Brazilian and Albanian-British co-production, according to her record label. She said she wanted to sing both in her native Spanish and in English in order to touch as many hearts as possible with her music (which, of course, also means increased sales). For Sofia, this was an exciting writing challenge (a 'beautiful' one, as she says), which she did in collaboration with Anitta (a Brazilian whose full name is Larissa de Macedo Machado) and Rita Ora (who was born Rita Sahatçiu, in Kosovo). She sees working across cultures as an enriching experience that she likes to promote. Sofia has swiftly become the biggest Mexican artist on Spotify. Her videos have attracted more than 600 million YouTube views and she's been featured on BBC Radio 1's Best New Pop playlist.

And many other artists have also been inspired to use languages creatively as a source of sounds and patterns, or even to make up words and phrases. The Icelandic band Sigur Rós are well known for lacing their lyrics with made-up emotive vocals that they call 'hopelandic' (*vonlenska* in Icelandic). On their website's FAQ page they steer away from the idea that this is meant to be an actual language (with words and grammar); instead they use sounds that match the mood of their music.

This brings us nicely to the world of language creators, whom we visit next.

Language 'nerds'

In the realm of virtual worlds, the designers of new languages ('conlangers') attract considerable attention. One of them is David Peterson, who was chosen to devise the entire Dothraki language for the TV series *Game of Thrones*, based on the few words and phrases used in George R. R. Martin's original book series *A Song of Ice and Fire*. A leading member of the Language Creation Society, David explained to the BBC in 2019 that when making up a language, he starts by imagining how the language might sound before moving on to building up a grammar structure around it.[51] David's fascination with conlangs means that he sees creating more of them as his life's mission. Always keen to convey his passion to the actors that will use his languages, David works with them over the phone or by Skype.

There are other constructed languages that have developed their own cultural appeal too. One of them, Klingon, from Star Trek, has an enormous following. The Klingon Language Institute provides language proficiency certification for learners, as well as producing its own publications.

Away from TV, many video game designers construct their own languages for their make-believe worlds, with an eye to attracting followers in that part of the entertainment industry. One prominent example is the fantasy video game series *Dragon Age*, where role playing includes use of the fictional languages Ander and Tevene.

And then there are those who engage with others in conlangs simply for recreational purposes. As Oliver Mayeux, a linguist and conlang enthusiast who draws inspiration from his knowledge of various dialects and Creole languages, says:[52]

> *It's like poetry or painting – people who do it have a natural expressiveness and admiration for language. We don't do it for fame or notoriety, we're a rather eccentric tribe of language nerds, coming together to discuss their creations.*

Linguists

Many conlangers have drawn on actual linguists for their inspiration. The grandmaster of made-up languages is the English philologist and author J. R. R. Tolkien (1892–1973). He was keen to understand the origins and development of a spoken tongue, and this led him to create his own languages that he embedded in fantastic mythologies. As well as his creation Elvish, Sauron's Black Speech can also be found in *Lord of the Rings*. Tolkien might have been surprised to hear that his languages featured in a cinematic blockbuster. He felt that one should learn a language for the love of it, not for its practical or economic purpose. Though he knew several 'real' languages (possibly as many as twenty), he is known to have used them rarely for communication.

It was a different vision that inspired Ludwik Lejzer Zamenhof (1859–1917) to create Esperanto: a neutral language that he hoped would unite rather than divide. This language needed to be different from others but easy to learn, so that everyone could use it. In constructing it, he drew on his knowledge of other languages including Yiddish, Russian, Polish, German, French, Latin, Greek, Hebrew and Aramaic. In the end, Esperanto did not become the universal communication tool its creator had hoped for, but it still boasts a following of about two million speakers worldwide as well a presence on Google Translate (as did Klingon until recently).[53]

Dealing with challenges

Polyglots can be found in all walks of life. Among citizens whose language skills can make a difference in a multilingual context are those who casually connect people, those who witness a crime and even individuals who save lives, which is what young Adul Sam-on did.

Citizen interpreter

Adul Sam-on was one of a group of teenage footballers who entered the Tham Luang cave in northern Thailand on 23 June 2018. While they were underground, the monsoon rains hit, flooding their narrow underground passage. The boys were stranded, with no food, during the time they were trapped inside the cave. Nine days into their ordeal they were starting to lose patience and hope, and they were low in physical energy. It was at that critical moment that an expedition led by two British divers located the group four kilometres from the entrance.

When the divers finally reached the boys, they shone a torch at them and asked: 'How many of you?' Adul, the only English-speaker in the group, greeted them and replied in a faint but clear voice: 'thirteen'.[54] So it was that during a protracted rescue effort, in difficult circumstances, Adul took on an unexpected leadership role as a casual interpreter. His personal intervention was instrumental in the operation that rescued the boys.

It turned out that Adul was growing up in poverty on the porous border between Thailand and Myanmar and Laos, where diverse populations intersect.[55] A speaker of Chinese, Burmese, Thai and his native Wa language, he had also picked up some English. Born in Wa, a region under dispute within Myanmar, he was stateless. His parents had 'slipped' him into Thailand when he was just six years old to protect him from conflict, to allow him to get an education and to give him opportunities that were unavailable in his home state.

Under the trying circumstances in that flooded cave, it was Adul's ease with languages that helped him and his friends to be saved. He then started a new life, subsequently being awarded a full scholarship to a college preparatory boarding school in New York. The Thai government also eventually granted him citizenship in recognition of his achievements.

As my selection of notable linguists suggests, speaking several languages can lay a foundation for much of what an individual becomes. We have already seen how people have always benefitted from knowing languages, enabling them to travel and trade with distant partners, to learn about new techniques, to invent, to influence and to govern.

Many inventors and scientists have also combined their curiosity about the world with their knowledge of multiple languages, a great example being Nobel Prize winner Marie (Skłodowska) Curie. A Polish French-naturalized physicist, Curie earned two Nobels in different disciplines (one for physics in 1903, and one for chemistry in 1911) for her pioneering work on radioactivity and the discovery of the elements radium and polonium.

Countless other thinkers and creative individuals were at ease with different languages too: Mahatma Gandhi, for example, and Pablo Picasso, Friedrich Engels and Karl Marx, whose multilingual daughter Eleanor became a highly regarded translator and political activist.

Many translators in turn also became influencers. The theologian Martin Luther changed the Western world with his translation of the Bible (in 1522), which also facilitated the emergence of a standard for the German language that speakers of the many diffuse dialects used at that time could understand. Similarly, Queen Elizabeth I of England (1533–1602) left a legacy not only as a multilingual but also as a translator: of Cicero, Seneca and Calvin into English; and of religious work into Latin, French and Italian.

Astute leaders also use their languages for political intelligence, and we have evidence of this from antiquity. Cleopatra, the last ruling Pharaoh of ancient Egypt (69–30 BCE), was known for her prowess in strategically deploying her skills in (around) ten languages to extend her power while also consolidating her domestic strength.

We get a sense of how all these individuals drew on their multilingual capacity as one of many core skills in their portfolio, to converse, translate, interpret, negotiate and develop diplomatic relationships. Similarly, there are countless other journalists, civil servants, educationalists, businesspeople and peacekeepers who use the languages they know to make a difference to their lives and missions.

In the next chapter, we'll look into the role that you could play in meeting society's language needs.

CHAPTER 5

What can I do with languages?

WE'VE ALREADY SEEN THAT LANGUAGES can open doors to many opportunities, and often in unexpected ways. Looking ahead, you may be wondering whether languages can enhance your employment prospects. A quick internet search will reveal that the answer is yes! A typical example of what you might find appeared on the website Cudoo in December 2019: 'Top bilingual jobs in 2020' lists a range of options – from paramedic to bank teller – for people with a background in languages.[56] Could that cohort one day also include you?

You'll notice that the needs of employers when it comes to people's language skills vary considerably. Some job profiles list this ability as 'essential', while others describe it as merely 'desirable'. This means that there are openings in the job market for proficient multilinguals as well as for those who just know a few key words and phrases in another language, which they may have the chance to build on during the course of their employment.

While browsing job postings, you'll quickly discover that employers are often looking for people who are good communicators. They want individuals with creative mindsets, who are curious and flexible, who work well as part of a team, who can problem solve and who are willing to take risks. And in fact, these soft skills are among the ten most highly valued across all occupations. They're listed separately from language skills, but – as you may remember from Chapter 3 – being adaptable, communicative, creative and good at problem solving are all common characteristics of bilinguals.

Now let's hear from some young professionals about how they've benefitted from their knowledge of languages. As we shall see, they all enjoy flexibility in their lines of work. Being bilingual has allowed them to travel and find employment in multiple locations, in jobs ranging from international aid to banking, IT and entertainment.

Working in organizations

Hannah Clark graduated with a degree in Hispanic studies, but she didn't set out in that direction. At school, her teachers failed to inspire her, and as a result her route into languages was rocky. But during a family visit to Colombia she discovered what had previously been hidden from her: languages weren't just another school subject, they were also about people. Her lived experience overseas meant she was now able to see that languages were alive and had cultural depth, which made them more real.

This insight opened her eyes, dispelling the memories of her fruitless attempts to learn languages at school; it wasn't that she was no good at them, she realized, but that she hadn't been enthused by them in the classroom. While at university she travelled to Brazil, doing charity work in a favela. This experience kindled a desire to do international aid work – something that is relatively well paid. After graduation she lived in Mozambique and in the Amazon, where she trained local indigenous groups in the use of technology to help them fight for their rights. As she told *The Guardian* in 2013,[57] she understands that languages have an important social dimension and she uses them as a means to connect with people in need.

In moving from charity work to international aid, Hannah will have been asked to perform more specialized tasks, which will have sharpened her language and humanitarian skills too. With her knowledge of Spanish and Portuguese, she's well placed for assignments in parts of the world where these languages are spoken as a legacy of past colonial ties. Her campaign work also sees her linking up with a network of local individuals to translate their recorded information into the area's major indigenous languages.

Hannah has what it takes to thrive in international development. She displays resilience through her willingness to live under challenging conditions, in regions where she can interact with people in their own languages. Her decision to switch from voluntary work to positions of considerable responsibility shows that she's open to change and keen to learn fresh skills in order to meet the requirements of her new roles.

Millennials now represent a large fraction of the overall workforce, and statistics show that they are likely to change careers an average of five to seven times during their working lives.[58] Flexibility and adaptability are consequently seen as standard requirements in twenty-first-century workplaces. Employers are on the look out for people like Hannah: people who are versatile and who have a positive attitude that breeds increased productivity and greater resilience.

With her commitment to people's needs in far-away places and her knowledge of three widely used languages (English, Spanish and Portuguese), there are many other challenging settings in which Hannah might excel: as a disaster relief worker, for example. These first responders react to crises such as floods, droughts and conflict, or outbreaks of diseases such as Ebola or Covid-19, in countries across the globe. Hannah already has the required cultural awareness and language ability, which are considered as important as good judgment and tact in this line of work. Alternatively, in another life, and with more training back at home, Hannah might instead have gone into teaching, translating or interpreting: areas on which we now focus.

Interpreting and translating

The services of translators and interpreters are needed in many different settings, with a range of languages being valued. The huge number of non-English speakers on the move around the world mean that demand for these specialists is expected to increase. If you are attracted to community interpreting in the UK, you'll need to have acquired linguistic skills through study, experiential practice or focused learning, and you'll need a diploma in order to work in Public Services Interpreting (see Chapter 7). Here, you provide a specialized service across multiple locations. Your task is to facilitate access to, and use of, the justice system (the courts, solicitors, immigration), local government (housing, social work, education) and health services (hospitals, clinics, GP practices) for people whose first language is not English.

More specifically, bilingual professionals are required for a range of tasks in many different areas of public life. The courts depend on interpreting services in evidential work (related to a persecution, for example: interviewing detainees, victims and witnesses, or taking statements). Another major employer of people from various language backgrounds is the London Metropolitan Police. The Met is a vast organization and it needs bilingual officers who are capable of developing a rapport with the city's diverse citizens in frontline policing, to foster good community relations and to manage public order (e.g. at football matches). The military also depends on language professionals, to interpret for British personnel stationed overseas, and the security services need them to help with terrorism detection and in the battle against transnational organized crime.

Another option could be to join the emergency services, dealing with callers who are asking for urgent medical assistance or police protection, relaying instructions to first responders on the ground, such as firefighters, police officers and ambulance drivers. There is also a demand for bilingual paramedics – who play a vital role in emergency healthcare services, delivering effective frontline care – and for medical interpreters in the hospital setting.

And being bilingual in the healthcare sector opens up job prospects in other parts of the world, too. You could seek out the opportunities available for language experts as frontline responders with programmes such as Médecins Sans Frontières (Doctors

Without Borders) and Aid for Africa, or you could look for work in organizations such as UNICEF or the World Health Organization. Or how about Translators without Borders, set up to ensure that information reaches people in the languages they speak, saving lives in times of crisis.

Working in the civil service

Languages feature among the fundamental skills required for overseas postings, especially for diplomats. They are so important, in fact, that the Foreign, Commonwealth & Development Office (FCDO) in London offers officials training in around 70 languages (ranging from Arabic to Zulu). Let's look at the story of a diplomat we'll call Josh,[59] who initially specialized in Farsi, reaching a good operational level in the language (he reached level C2; for more information, see Chapter 7). His story is that of an aspiring professional intent on engaging deeply in foreign relations. As he explained to me in a recent phone conversation:

> *You have to be intellectually curious in this job, you need to want to make these connections because if you don't make them while you are overseas, I don't see where is the value that you add. You have to have local insights and expertise, so you need the language. Without it you don't have the local touch. ... You cannot properly understand a place culturally unless you speak the language. I think it's so intertwined with the cultural references from language. Also, when you learn a language you don't learn it purely in isolation, there is always some other kind of reference, culture, history, media, so I think through language you get more insights.*

Josh's decision to learn Farsi was driven by a combination of factors: an opportunity to do so was advertised internally at the FCDO, and he already had a taste for the Persian culture and a bit of the language because one of his best friends from university was brought up speaking Farsi. What is more, professionally speaking, Iran is an interesting region to work on. During the course of his training, the UK's relationship with Iran was difficult: diplomacy was hopefully the way forward.

After later being assigned a post in Bucharest, Josh and his young family embarked on learning Romanian. This was important for him, as a diplomat, because often his key interlocuters in meetings were older people, who weren't confident enough to use English. Knowing the language also helped him in his interactions with the media.

Josh now finds himself posted to Berlin, and he's ready to tackle German next. He says that learning languages serves as a useful tool for building trust in his line of work. His view is that

> *human beings have a natural inclination to distrust 'the other'. Language is a very clear way that we differentiate between the other and us. If people show willingness to try and bridge that gap, this goes a long way. Also, since we [diplomats] are in the business [of working] with people and forming connections, languages can help do that.*

It is natural, then, that developing skills in languages is a central requirement in foreign relations. In the FCDO, diplomats are incentivized to learn languages by awards and wage bonuses, so those with ambition tend to be, or become, good linguists. Josh gets paid more because he knows Farsi, and he appreciates that recognition because, he says, learning it was hard. More significantly, he comes across as someone who genuinely cherishes languages per se, and as a tool for forming a genuine rapport with people and their culture.

Effective communication is clearly a priority for community support, such as in the healthcare and social work sectors, in foreign relations and, as we shall see below, in customer-led services across a range of industries. Moreover, in the UK people who can read and write Gaelic or Welsh, in addition to English, are also in demand for employment in government, the civil service and in publishing.

But maybe you're thinking of studying mathematics, science or engineering. If so, developing technical skills and knowledge will clearly be your priority. Perhaps you're wondering whether languages, and the associated essential soft skills, are also seen as significant here? In fact, professionals with an aptitude in languages are highly valued by a range of companies, including those in the finance sector. In the next job profile we look at, we'll see how combining science with language study worked out successfully for one former student.

Joining a business

You don't always need to have concentrated entirely on language study to be desirable to employers who are looking for bilingual capability. Many universities offer a range of accredited language options in different combinations with other subjects. And it was this path that appealed to Jacob Gilbert, who chose to study mathematics with a language before embarking on a career with the Royal Bank of Scotland.

Jacob had always liked languages at school, but he wanted to study 'something mathematical'.[60] When he did his research, though, he found that there were universities that offered mathematics and languages as a joint degree (as we shall see in Chapter 7, this means that both subjects were studied to the same depth, i.e. language study is not an add-on).

Even when every other student on his course had dropped the language element by the end of the first year, Jacob carried on, spending his year abroad in Spain – and he considers it one of the best decisions he's ever made. The extra effort of combining mathematics and a language turned out to be a good investment, too. His time in Spain obviously helped him with speaking the language, but the cultural insights he gathered also enabled him to get on with people from different backgrounds. It was these personal skills that stood out when he applied for a post in the finance sector and received a job offer.

Jacob's joint studies have equipped him with a great combination of essential skills: hard/technical and soft/communication. This is a highly valued skillset, much sought after by employers. As he sees it, the technical abilities and knowledge he brings to bear in order to successfully execute his responsibilities are only part of what makes him the best he can be within his organization. He knows that it is thanks to his communication skills that he is able to effectively work with others in his workplace, enabling him to pass on his project findings in non-technical terms both to colleagues and to management.

In addition, as many business leaders know, a multicultural workforce is a key resource that can yield creative benefits that add value in business. Workplace observations show that language-diverse teams often produce original solutions to practical problems. This is thought to happen because speakers of different languages have different mental models of the world, and they have their own distinctive way of expressing ideas.[61] All this means that numerous employers are on the look out for a multilingual talent pool. Many companies also seek out human resources professionals with competence in different languages to help them bring on board workers from diverse language backgrounds.

Communicating across cultures
Jacob's appreciation of Hispanic culture is an asset for his company. Not only is he able to communicate with clients in their primary

language (demonstrating respect), but he also understands their traditions and ways of thinking. This all means that he brings to his job an awareness of how cultural differences can affect cross-border interactions and outcomes: a skill that is much valued by employers in the international marketplace.

Everyone engaged in international business knows that effective communication – both verbal and non-verbal – is key to successful commercial relationships. It is vital for professionals to have some awareness of how other cultures view essential values: time etiquette, for example, and what is and isn't considered polite. From your first encounter with someone from another culture, you'll already be conveying your personal signature. As a Westerner in China, for example, you must not offer too firm a handshake: it could be construed as a sign of aggression. In Japan, bowing is an important gesture. The deeper and longer the bow, the stronger the respect and emotion displayed, but gauging the correct form and duration depends on fully understanding the personal relationship that the bow acknowledges. Many companies provide their employees with training – in thanking clients, or apologizing; in making a request, or asking someone a favour – so they get such customs right. Having an understanding of such cultural nuances builds mutual respect, which will in turn benefit business.

Successful communication is not, therefore, simply a question of using words appropriately. Companies want versatile employees who can speak different languages and who are also able to navigate different cultural expectations. A recent survey report from the Economist Intelligence Unit[62] on how cultural and language barriers affect business confirms that effective cross-border communication and collaboration are critical to the financial success of companies with international aspirations. Richard Hardie, former chairman of the investment bank UBS, has been quoted as saying that international companies require employees with a profound knowledge and appreciation of the cultural nuances and tone of languages, in order to 'cajole and seduce' clients to act in such a way as to do things that they would not otherwise do.[63]

Multilingual astuteness and intercultural sensitivity are especially critical at the negotiating table, where miscommunication can derail a deal or spoil a potential partnership. Knowing and respecting your partner's culture will go a long way towards establishing trust. Trust in this context is linked to the way we experience cultures and languages and requires both language know-how and cultural intelligence.

Customer service

> *If I'm selling to you, I speak your language. But if I'm buying, dann müssen Sie Deutsch sprechen [then you have to speak German].*

This quote – often attributed to Willy Brandt, a former Chancellor of the Federal Republic of Germany – alludes to customers' rights. Sales are more likely when potential buyers can get information in their own language about products they're interested in. This is why many international businesses strategically invest in people with competence in different languages: to boost consumer interest and, ultimately, profit. After all, this approach is not new: the ancient traders we followed in Chapter 2 already knew this.

Companies today serve increasingly diverse, multilingual populations, both at home and abroad. They therefore depend on quality service provision across a range of languages. This is another reason why businesses see it as a top priority to have multi-language ability represented among their staff. Customer service representatives with such skills are in demand for handling queries and complaints from diverse callers. As the first line of communication with customers, they work to eliminate language barriers with callers who do not speak English. By developing a multilingual, outward-facing skills pool, companies seek to grow their customer base and retain loyalty.

Historically, provision of such language services has often been outsourced to centres overseas, where lower costs used to be charged for this type of work. But many companies have recently begun to relocate their call centres closer to home, partly because of rising rates in the various service delivery regions around the world, but also as a result of cultural incompatibilities that can occur in such work. All in all, the strong demand for professionals with multiple language capabilities to satisfy worldwide communication needs has engendered a booming trade globally, as well as closer to home.

Doing communications engineering

Some university entrants seize the opportunity to learn a new language from scratch. Tanya, a former student of mine who studied electrical and electronic engineering at Bristol University, had done French at school and decided to take up an Italian language option as a fresher.[64] Both languages would in due course prove to shape her early career.

Following graduation, Tanya soon found herself working in the Rome headquarters of Leonardo SpA, one of the largest defence contractors in the world. After her personal circumstances changed, she was offered a posting with Airbus in Toulouse. She now had to switch from Italian to French: a tall order when her grounding in the latter came all the way back in her school days. She found herself attached to a mixed-language group, working on the company's pilot–controller communication system, which provides pilots with regular updates on the condition of their aircraft. Now fully immersed in French, she quickly refreshed and extended her knowledge of the language.

Having demonstrated that she is capable of adapting well to new places, Tanya's skills will be highly valued in the international market, where engineering services are most required. As we saw in Chapter 1, French will open doors to jobs in many Francophone parts of the world: in the Caribbean and in Africa, for example, where ten countries have French as their official language. France has a string of successful businesses around the globe, and many French-Canadian organizations also work with companies in the northeastern US.

Engineers are needed in most walks of life: from product design to building construction, from IT to communication. Graduates with language skills can therefore be expected to find employment in any engineering area in almost any part of the world. For example, some of the fastest-growing markets in the Arabic-speaking Middle East are busy investing in their infrastructure, with numerous ground-breaking engineering projects on the go. There are also plenty of lucrative engineering jobs opening up as a result of China's intercontinental 'Belt and Road' initiative.

Localization

Communication is essential in any line of work, and modern communication is complicated as well as important, particularly in an international context. It uses different forms of textual, visual and cultural (multimodal) literacy and involves intercultural intelligence.

An entire, largely internet-driven, sector has evolved to deliver language support to organizations and enterprises intent on adapting their products and services for domestic and international customers. In this line of business, bilingual professionals with advanced software skills are needed for the purpose of delivering information and for multilingual communication. Their expertise is sought after by companies planning to export to new countries, so they can ensure that the specifications of their products and services meet the conventions and expectations of the targeted foreign markets. This also means adapting the tone, voice, concepts and images used in (online) advertising in a culturally appropriate and sensitive way without causing misunderstandings or offence among prospective consumers. Lessons have been learned from misfiring product launches, as happened when the Scandinavian vacuum cleaner manufacturer Electrolux tried to advertise its goods in the US with the slogan 'Nothing sucks like an Electrolux'.

In response to rising demand, technology firms are looking to bilinguals with various specializations to help them with their product development and customer service. Data scientists, who are part of this growing industry, need mathematics and statistics knowledge, substantive language expertise, and also soft skills that are seen as characteristics of linguists. These interpersonal skills include flexibility (of mind) and, as we have seen, an ability to work creatively in multi-language teams. Individuals who, like Tanya, are able to marry their language and intercultural capabilities with their programming and engineering skills are therefore in high demand.

Machine translation

Technology goes a long way towards eliminating cultural barriers and enhancing global cooperation, but it does not obviate the need for human communication. Machine translation is based on statistics and artificial intelligence, and it works by choosing the most *probable* translation. It cannot, therefore, replace the quintessential human touch. As pointed out earlier, it works by decoding text rather than by understanding it. Although speech recognition is becoming more sophisticated, any conversation with your smart speaker will quickly show that this mode of interaction is hardly nuanced.

It takes a human translator – with feelings and creativity, and the ability to pick up the subtleties and deep meanings of communication – to reproduce the tone, colour and vibrancy of the original text in a new language. The origin of this problem lies with the idea that different languages encode different views of the world. For example, if you say 'it is raining cats and dogs' in English, the literal translation into any other language will be met with incredulity. Sure, you can teach any translation system to override the decoding. But what if you'd instead said that you could 'murder a sandwich'?

Aside from the obvious problem of decoding versus understanding, monolingual users of translation technology will not be in a position to grasp the subtleties of interactions. They won't know what gets lost in translation either, whether it's carried out electronically or by humans. As we have seen, there's plenty of evidence that language gaps can have adverse effects in export markets, where misunderstandings have stood in the way of major cross-border transactions, incurring significant losses for companies. These tangible examples of key trade negotiations that have become lost in translation point to the need for languages in business.

Professionals with multi-language competencies will always be required in this industry, not least to check on mistranslations. An amusing recent example occurred in a supermarket in Wales. The shop had had a sign printed to advertise its alcohol-free drinks section. As you can see in Figure 11, the English was written correctly. However, as the Welsh speakers among you will realize, the translation was incorrectly rendered as 'free alcohol'.[65] One Twitter user, Guto Aaron, was quick off the mark. On spotting the sign, he tweeted: 'Get yourself to Asda, according to their dodgy Welsh translations they are giving away free alcohol.' This example shows that bilingual speakers are indispensable in ensuring that the right message is being conveyed.

Figure 11 Alcohol-free or free alcohol? That depends on whether you're speaking English or Welsh. (Photograph reproduced with kind permission of Guto Aaron (@GutoA).)

In summary, we have seen that software professionals with a background in languages are always an asset in IT, whether it is in communications, customization or machine translation. Moreover, in the realms of art and entertainment, where formal qualifications are not the norm, knowing languages and other cultures can provide benefits when it comes to creative input on top of delivering organizational advantages, as we'll see below.

Performing arts and entertainment

The creative aspect of languages is widely seen in the world of entertainment. Languages and cultures are fertile source material for innovative use in films, digital animations, theatre and music: all the way from the inspiration and production stages through to the final performance. Many multilingual artists are involved in these pursuits.[66] They may have absorbed languages as part of their heritage or learned them through education, travel or collaboration.

A striking example is the recent rise of K-pop, part of South Korea's vibrant cultural scene. Many of the genre's young artists master several different languages (mostly Korean and English, but also Mandarin, Thai and Japanese[67]), which they then knit into their lyrics. They also use their languages to communicate with an international fanbase, both through their music and online. K-pop's idols have swiftly become worldwide phenomena, even charting in the West. Fans who don't know (much) Korean use 'translation accounts' on Twitter when they want to understand 'the content (of) their favourite artists' posts'.[68] In promoting multilingual music in this way, these young performers are kick-starting the use of more diverse languages in song. Here's a vivid example of the popularity of many artists relying on their language abilities. If this westward cultural wave continues, the K-pop industry may well go on to stimulate interest in Korean as a language to learn in the Occident.

Similarly, many inspired young individuals based in the West use different languages – and, relatedly, different cultural ideas – as part of their creative work. A recent report in the UK, for example, carries interviews with groups of young artists from the West Midlands who employ the various languages they know in spoken, performance and visual arts, and in filmmaking, painting and writing.[69] With family backgrounds from diverse parts of the world (Arabic-speaking regions, India, Africa, Poland, the Caribbean), they bring into play combinations of language resources (including slang and dialect) that are related to their heritage, showing us different ways of thinking and communicating. The innovative work of these young artists with the resources emanating from their language-diverse personal histories turn them into culturally inspired ambassadors who add value socially as well as making a contribution to the economy.

The creative industry itself has become a thriving engine for the circulation of cultural products, both online and offline. It is a sector that depends on expert input from the people who, through a combination of imagination and technical know-how, generate our make-believe worlds. Professionals with coding skills as well as multi-language competencies are highly sought after to produce user-friendly platforms for virtual collaboration, entertainment and learning. Among the many online environments that are being created you'll also find a wide range of language education tools that enjoy a growing market. Connecting language learning with social networking, hobbies, special interests and gaming, programmers work to provide audiovisual sceneries for immersive experiences in which languages are practised interactively, while at the same time stimulating a learner's enjoyment and amusement.

The languages bonus

Speaking a second language yields numerous benefits. It brings gains at every level: professionally, socially and personally. Clearly, you cannot find employment as a translator or an interpreter without the necessary language skills, but equally, whether you work in education, science, finance, tourism, communication or entertainment, you'll have limitations if you are monolingual.

And the converse is true, too: with more than just one language, you'll face fewer obvious restrictions in other careers. Diplomats and politicians can be much more influential when they're able to operate in different languages. Advertisers will be more successful when they have local and regional market knowledge. Business-people are likely to do better if they can speak the language of their counterparts abroad. In virtually all areas of work, being multilingual is an advantage.

Business executive Lucy Jeynes has written engagingly about how knowing languages has benefitted her career.[70] She studied French at university, and at first sight, an understanding and appreciation of French novels doesn't necessarily seem like the best preparation for a high-flying business career. But in her chosen profession of facilities management, she soon discovered that the experiences she had gained through her studies helped her appreciate cultural cues in a job where hard, technical skills are traditionally more highly valued.

In Chapter 3 we saw how knowledge of the mechanics of another language can carry over to your primary language. In the same way, Lucy found that her degree helped her to formulate ideas more clearly in English: both her writing (proposals, press releases, etc.) and her speaking (conference presentations, negotiations, etc.) were enhanced, especially when it came to discussing complex technical details with her engineering colleagues.

To sum up, knowing another language won't only enhance your career prospects, it will also add value to your personal life. Languages are a key to knowledge, and they can boost our intelligence. Learning languages leads to more opportunities, and helps you to know a variety of cultures and ways of life. As active citizens in a globalizing world, what we need is to be able to read, understand and debate the key issues that affect us all every day.

Let us now move on to look at ways of learning languages.

CHAPTER 6

How do you study languages?

WE'VE SEEN THAT LEARNING A new language is a very individual venture. We all draw on different motivations when we make our choices in life. So what drives *you* to learn a language? What are *your* ambitions? What do *you* want to do in life? Where are *you* planning to go? Maybe you're not yet sure what you want to do after you've completed your education, but you do know that you like learning languages.

Chances are that you may already have some idea about which language interests you, whether you realize it or not. You may like the way it sounds, or the culture that is associated with it, or the fact that some of your family speak it. But how do you actually get into learning it? What are your personal learning goals? What resources are you able to draw on?

Crucially, you need to think about what type of learner you are. Are you an auditory learner, who soaks up the musicality of a language? Or are you a note taker or a practical learner, thriving through doing? Are you an externally driven pragmatist, an internally propelled idealist, or a 'perseverer': someone who will tackle anything that comes their way? Perhaps you already know another language? Such experience could smooth your path.

Let us now rejoin some of the individuals we met in Chapter 4. On reading their life stories earlier on in this book, you may well have noticed that they all had strong incentives to learn and that they came across as self-propelled learners. Their voices ring with determination and promise. Perhaps they might fire your imagination.

Knowing and learning languages

Because you can easily get hold of publications on the technicalities of language learning, you won't find such details on the pages that follow. Instead, we'll go on a journey of reflection about you as a learner and look at the way language studies connect with the person you are and how you see the world. I will introduce three learner types below. You may see yourself as sharing characteristics with one or more of the categories, and I hope you'll gain some deeper understanding of what drives you in your language-learning decision.

The idealist

Are you an idealist by temperament, passionate about personal growth and development? Are you enthusiastic about the choices you make and trust your intuition when it comes to making them? If so, you might share some traits with Jhumpa Lahiri, the author we met in Chapter 4, whose steps we shall now retrace.

Casting your mind back to Jhumpa, you'll recall how she explained that growing up with two languages was fraught with conflict. There was Bengali, her home language, and English, the language of her education and of her American friends after her family moved to the US when Jhumpa was a child. In her *Observer* article, she tells of her regret that her mother's tongue, Bengali, which she can speak but not read or write, is not her primary language.[71]

It was down to serendipity that Jhumpa stumbled upon a language that eventually dispelled the dilemmas she had experienced growing up. She says that the moment she met Italian (in 1994, on a trip to Florence with her sister) was, for her, like a bolt of lightning (*un colpo di fulmine*).[72] Perhaps the language also sounded familiar to her because of its similarities to Latin, which Jhumpa had learned at school.

She followed her impulse to develop a relationship with what was to become her third (living) language. Along the way, her love of the language grew ever more intense. When she eventually came to pen her reflections, she confessed that giving in to this desire to learn Italian became her infatuation, her devotion, even her obsession (*infatuazione, devozione, ossessione*).[73]

Jhumpa has also spoken of her desire to know other languages, too. She regrets not being able to speak Hindi when she visits India, for instance. Doing so would naturally be an immersive experience for her, since she feels that 'learning a language is the most profound thing we can do'.[74] In the pages that follow we'll witness her developing an intense intimacy with – and deep respect towards – Italian.

The pragmatist

Do you like to be practical and get on with doing what works best in your life? Are you logical, and focused on reaching a goal? Do you prefer real-world applications of ideas to abstract notions? This describes the mindset of Matthias Maurer, the trainee astronaut we met earlier, whom we are now going to rejoin.

Matthias has a strong external incentive to steadfastly pursue his language studies. He knows that joint action in space demands an ability to communicate with fellow astronauts, as he explains in an interview in *The Linguist*:[75] 'Until it is clear which will be my path [as a spaceman], I need to train in all the language skills.'

But it has not been plain sailing. Matthias could already speak English and French, so learning Italian and Spanish wasn't terribly difficult. Chinese and Russian were harder though, and he found that he struggled. At the time of writing, Matthias is hoping to be selected for a place on the planned Chinese space station.[76] He knows that investing time and effort in learning Chinese is mission critical for him.

This story illustrates how focus is fundamental as we strive towards our aims in life. For Matthias, learning and knowing languages is not an insurmountable hurdle to his aspiration to play a key role as an astronaut in a space mission. Driven by pragmatic, instrumental values and strategically developing his language experiences, he is preparing himself to achieve his ambition. A self-efficacious learner, he has set challenging goals for himself and is determined to achieve them. Above all, he's willing to take risks and he enjoys the experience of mastering new languages through an activity he loves.

The reflective 'perseverer'

Are you someone who never gives up, regardless of any obstacles that may be put in your way? Do you carry on with a task because you believe in it – because it has meaning for you? Are you reflective about the resilience you develop in life?

For Martina Navratilova, getting used to English was a matter of great urgency when she moved to the US as a rising tennis star. She says that adapting to the language was easy. She already had a background in Russian and Latin, both of which she liked, finding them enjoyably complex languages. She had learned them at school, alongside French, which she thought of as tuneful. She has tried to keep in touch with her native Czech, which is no longer her primary language, but she has sometimes found herself searching for words when speaking it, even having to translate from English.[77]

Her no-nonsense approach to life means she is practical about her use of languages. If she makes a mistake, she wants someone to correct her. Whether on or off court, she is intent on learning by doing, always striving to become better. She knows that the insights she gains from her errors will help her to improve – in languages as in tennis.

Finally, it needn't be love for a particular activity or culture that inspires someone to embark on a language-learning journey: sometimes it can be love for a special person. In the case of English-speaking Lauren Collins, a self-confessed monoglot, it was a deepening romance that enticed her to become a late-life bilingual. Failing to learn French – the language of her husband-to-be – was not an option for her. She decided early on that she didn't want to be isolated from his community, and the couple would eventually bring up their daughter bilingually. For Lauren, knowing French became a resource: an intellectual investment.

Her linguistic love story is the subject of her recent memoir *When in French: Love in a Second Language*.[78] The book covers Lauren's transformative midlife journey of becoming bilingual and her experience of loving someone who speaks another language. In her reflections she wonders whether two people can really get close to each other if they don't share each other's language. Does 'I love you' even mean the same thing as '*Je t'aime*'? And how about striking up a relationship with someone in whose language this sentiment cannot be expressed in that manner?

And there are in fact many different ways of conveying this intimate emotion in different languages. Let's look at some examples just from the languages (in addition to French) that are used in my family. In Ilocano (a language spoken in the Philippines), the word 'love' is rarely used. Tamil (mainly used in Sri Lanka) has words for 'love' (*anpu* or *kathal*), but it doesn't have an everyday phrase for 'I love you'. Instead, a man would declare his love for someone more formally by saying '*naan ungalai kathalikkirean*', for 'I am in love with you'. Speakers use this phrase exclusively romantically (so not with their children, for example), but have many other terms of endearment of course.[79] Finally, in my native Swiss German (which consists of a group of dialects), you would traditionally say '*I ha di gärn*' (meaning 'I like you'). Standard (high) German, however, has '*Ich liebe dich*' or (the slightly weaker) '*Ich hab' dich lieb*'. A speaker of Swiss German, then, has to adapt when feeling moved to say 'I love you', '*je t'aime*' or '*ich liebe dich*'. Getting to know your partner's language is therefore also about learning to see the world through another pair of eyes.

We get a firm sense from the stories above that each protagonist's language goals resonate with their values. The way they perceive themselves and what drives them are powerful motors to learning. Each of the individuals embarked on their language-learning journey for a different reason. They were clear about why they wanted to study a language, and this anchored their motivation. One imagines that they set themselves manageable goals, knowing what they wanted to achieve, and possibly also by when.

As adults who had to fit their language quest around the demands of everyday life, they needed to be resourceful. We know that each of them started off by embarking on a spell of formal study. It was through personal instruction that they were initially able to create a human connection with the target language. In addition, contextual, skills-based activities will have helped them to cement the building blocks needed for measured progress. Along the way, they will also have drawn on various flexible, informal means of learning, using different materials and modes of interaction in their chosen language, both offline and online.

Combining different ways of learning

So what is the best way to learn? Can we improve our mode of learning as we take our language journey? How can we put our new knowledge and skills into practice? Let's look at some time-honoured truths from a period when we weren't surrounded by the multiplicity of resources that are available today.

When it comes to the basics of learning a language, the means that we deploy haven't changed much. Meet Sir Richard Francis Burton (1821–90), a dashing Victorian diplomat and adventurer, who is known to have learned lots of languages. As well as being able to accumulate different languages with ease through his travels, he had another special interest: erotic literature.[80] He wasn't afraid to go against the prevailing social mores of the time, as evidenced by his translation and publication of a collection of (sexually explicit) Arabic stories: a collection that later became known as *One Thousand and One Nights*.

Burton had developed his own way of learning languages. He is known to have said that, to begin with, he would learn simple grammar and vocabulary by heart, working in short bursts in order to keep his mind alert.[81] Then, once he'd amassed a few hundred basic words, he would tackle longer written pieces to augment his vocabulary and his understanding of sentence structures. And when he felt ready, he'd select a book that interested him, so that his progress would become more rapid.

These are clearly the notes of a self-driven learner: one whose method can perhaps best be summarized as

▶ note important words;
▶ learn the essential structures;
▶ practise useful phrases;
▶ study regularly, frequently and consistently, dividing the material into manageable chunks; and finally
▶ immerse yourself in the culture of your target language.[82]

The overall message conveyed here is: find the way of learning that suits you best and stick to it.

Burton's method reminds us that when learning a language, frequent use is more important than simply increasing the range of new words and structures we accumulate. In order to successfully store new knowledge in our brains over the long term, our learning needs to be regular and maintained at a certain level of intensity. The period when you're at school or university is a good time to take up another language because the part of the brain you use to absorb and organize new information – the cortex – is being heavily used during education.

There are, of course, a myriad of situations in which you can learn languages: at home, while travelling or when preparing to meet new people. Some individuals may perform better in an organized class-based setting and therefore opt for a language unit, perhaps alongside their main subject (see Chapter 7 on possible routes to pursue). This allows for concentrated effort at the start of your study, which is certainly optimal when it comes to acquiring the fundamentals of any new skill. Other people though, like Richard Burton, prefer a flexible, informal approach that links up with their life choices or special interests. Steady progress will be more likely if you combine both types of learning.

By whatever means you make progress, an awareness of the way in which you engage with your learning materials is key. Digital tools may help you anchor the elementary parts of your new language, but having free access to those tools will not in itself help you learn a language. You need to find out for yourelf what the best combination is for you. It's one thing to have a variety of resources to draw on, but another thing entirely to actively learn and retain new knowledge.

How did our author, trainee astronaut and sportswoman fit their language-learning activities into their busy lives?

Following her momentous first visit to Italy, Jhumpa Lahiri made several attempts to learn Italian by herself but failed to achieve any real progress. As she wrote much later, she simply wasn't sure how to get to grips with the language at that stage.[83] She describes feeling as if Italian, her new-found passion, didn't care about having her among its speakers; it was she who had to do all the work. To ease her way in, she ended up buying a book called *Teach Yourself Italian,*[84] but the book title only served to confirm that this way of learning is a lonely process. She felt cut off from the music of the language.

She needed to move on from being a lone learner, so she took up private lessons. Her vibrant and passionate teachers gave her vivid insights into the workings of Italian, but she continued to feel like she was operating outside the language, looking in, unsure how to say things, hesitant in her replies. In due course she came to realize that to truly *enter* the language, she needed to move to Italy. In preparation, six months before her departure, she commited to reading only in Italian, taking note of unfamiliar terms. As she wrote in an article in *The New Yorker*,[85] she felt she had to disconnect herself from her first language. By doing so, she was able to marvel fully at new words and grammar and to take joy whenever she overcame a difficulty, no matter how arduous the journey.

To anchor her new language's presence in her life while still in her native New York, she decided to immerse herself in it as she went about her days. She doesn't go into detail about how she does that, but one can imagine her trying to say things to herself in Italian or translate public notices on her way through the city (a technique that I'm personally familiar with). Jhumpa's language journey finds her covering all the basic approaches to language learning: listening and speaking, reading and writing, and translating.

With the European Space Agency seeing cooperation between no fewer than 23 member states, the language demands placed on Matthias Maurer are already complex. As we've said, it was clear to him that Chinese would be an important additional asset in his language repertoire.[86]

He learned the language in several phases. For the first few years, he took lessons from a speaker of Chinese. Then he was sent to the Bochum Language Institute, close to the ESA centre in Cologne, for

Chinese language training alongside other ESA staff. According to the *Linguist* article previously cited, he got 'very close to the B2 level' (again see Chapter 7) in just seven weeks of study, and he described the course as 'really intensive, really quick, really efficient'. After this general language programme, he took one-on-one classes that covered terminology that's essential for astronauts. In Matthias's own words, even once oral capacity is good, 'you need to (carry on working to) master the language. It's quickly learnt but also quickly forgotten.'

And there is still plenty for him to learn. He studied Chinese using Pinyin (a Romanized script of the Chinese characters based on their pronunciation), but this may not be enough to enable him to follow procedures once on board the Chinese space station:

> *If the procedure is only in [traditional] Chinese characters, that would make it really, really difficult. Imagine there's an emergency and you need to be very efficient, very fast, there shouldn't be errors at all.*

Martina Navratilova's entry into the world of big-time tennis came when she first went to the US for two months in 1973, aged 16 – this was her first time on the tour. She admits that she struggled with English at the time.[87]

Back home, in what was then Czechoslovakia, she continued in regular school. Once she began to travel more she enrolled at what was known as a school for working people: an institution for those who couldn't attend class on a daily basis. By the time she moved permanently to the US (aged 19), she was able to function in English as a professional tennis player.

From these language-learning portraits we can see that people will readily use a combination of methods, in formal and informal settings (and, in the case of Jhumpa, through partial immersion in the culture), to advance their knowledge. Online tools and websites, and possibly even social media, can provide additional, flexible support, and apps offer an opportunity to use repetition in order to anchor the declarative parts of a language (the words and phrases). Nevertheless, all our protagonists will have been aware that a clear method and a strong focus are more important to one's progress than the choice of learning tools. Using their selected resources with purpose, they will have built their consistency, with frequent and regular exposure to their new languages, and this may well become a life-long pursuit. For example, our diplomat Josh seized the opportunity presented by Britain's Covid-19 lockdown period to take private virtual lessons in Farsi, as he was beginning to feel a little rusty in that language.

Getting more experience

Becoming more deeply acquainted with another language requires time and effort, of course. As you immerse yourself in the culture of your target language, either virtually or physically, you start to embed your language skills, in much the same way as regular physical exercise improves your fitness. Immersion happens when you fully submerge yourself in the environment of the language you're learning, allowing you to acquire knowledge in an intuitive manner. This method doesn't primarily involve rules or explanations. It is instead a somewhat 'messy' – but also more holistic – stage of learning. One that engages all your senses, eventually recasting you, cognitively, emotionally, behaviourally. You are now learning more freely, through listening and watching; you are beginning to make associations of your own – as we'll see in the final part of our collection of real-life stories.

Once in Rome, Jhumpa Lahiri is ready to fully immerse herself in her new environment. In fact, she feels like she was fated to live there. So much so, in fact, that she starts to write her diary in Italian within a month of her arrival.

As she explains in her *New Yorker* piece,[88] this happened spontaneously. Despite being embarrassed by her initial attempts at writing falteringly in Italian, she decided to proceed intuitively, without the aid of a dictionary. At this stage, expressing herself in Italian seemed to her like some kind of trespassing, but also like part of a rebellious adventure. She knew she was facing an arduous task, and she compares her commitment to writing in her new language to ascending a mountain with the wrong equipment. Her pledge to do so felt like a 'literary act of survival'. Somehow, though, she finds her writing more genuine and her thoughts more continuous in Italian. The challenges she experiences with the language are, as she sees it, an opportunity for enrichment. Indeed, she discovered that she thrives when she encountered these language obstacles: making mistakes opened up new possibilities for discovery and exploration.

In Altre Parole (In Other Words), the first of what became a series of books she penned in Italian, is the result of her immersive experiment.[89] In it, she recounts her journey from English to Italian. In videos that she recorded for her publishers, she explains that she felt predestined to go to Rome: that imbuing herself with this new language had made her a different person and a better writer.[90]

The ESA currently uses a Soyuz launcher to get to the International Space Station. Matthias Maurer therefore decided to take himself to Saint Petersburg for a few weeks of intensive Russian language coaching.[91]

He was subsequently offered further training on the Soyuz aircraft, where, as he explains, 'all the controls and procedures ... are in Russian'.[92] Familiar with how space programmes work, he knew he couldn't rely long term on outside support with communication when on board the space capsule:

> *At first [we are helped by] an interpreter but then, as the trainee astronauts gain confidence in Russian, they are expected to do their spacecraft manning and survival drills without interpretation.*

At this stage, it's important that the crew train to work closely together, and they must try to ensure they really understand each other. Language immersion on a space capsule is intense, demanding precise communication both between crew members and when talking to ground staff. Every member of the team must be able to accurately use technical terminology when in contact with the Russian mission control centre.

For Josh, our diplomat from Chapter 5, learning Romanian effectively happened through immersion: by listening to interpreters in meetings, day in, day out. He says that studying Latin at school eased his path, since the two languages are related, and added:

> *I would quite regularly speak in English and someone would immediately interpret into Romanian. It's actually a very good way of learning a language. You hear what you wanted to say and then you hear it back in Romanian, and vice versa: you hear it in Romanian and then hear it translated into English.*

Through his daily interactions with his Romanian partners, his grasp of their language improved steadily, but it was still mostly confined to the work context. Nevertheless, becoming proficient in Romanian mattered to him as he finds that you miss out on detail, cues and asides when you use interpreters in a negotiation or meeting. Outside of that focused remit, such as when going shopping or ordering a meal in a restaurant, he did find that he would 'quite quickly run out of words'.

∿

These vivid examples show that learning a language is best achieved when one is surrounded by it, in the place where it is spoken. The constant stimulus your brain receives when using a new language every day forces it to embed, and ultimately means that you retain it better. An immersive period abroad helps you build up your language skills, absorb a new culture, meet people and become more self-reliant. It also enables you to extend your knowledge of your main subject through the language you are studying, as was the case with Jacob and Tanja (see Chapter 5).

Using your own resources

The language trajectories in the personal stories recounted above are often a lengthy process – things didn't happen overnight. The protagonists' starting points and their means of pursuing their aims varied, of course, but they all persevered in building on their language abilities. The primary characteristics that the stories share can serve as learning points for us: each of the people we've met already knew other languages, and they had an incentive to learn more. Also, they are actively using these languages, accumulating substantial personal language resources during the course of their lives.

Already knowing another language

It's often claimed that when someone already speaks more than one language it's easier to learn another. Why would this be so?

Could it be that they've gained confidence through their previous learning experience? Or perhaps they thrived as part of a language-diverse circle of friends? Maybe, having already ventured outside the confines of their primary language, they felt able to do so again?

Basically, what has been found to happen is that applying skills from one language to another uses a critical cognitive function that can make it easier to go through the learning process a second time.[93] In tackling a second language, you will develop knowledge, techniques and abilities that you didn't have before. And it is these gains that will, to some extent, be transferable to any other language you choose to learn next.

Another advantage of knowing multiple languages is that they can often reinforce one another. Most European languages have similar structures and many words in common (apart from Basque, which is an outlier, and the mutually linked trio of Hungarian, Estonian and Finnish). This is especially the case if they belong to the same language family, e.g. Slavic, Germanic or Latin-derived Romance.

So if, like Hannah from Chapter 5, you decide to learn Spanish and Portuguese, you'll be able to draw on their numerous shared characteristics as related (Romance) languages (though you'll have to guard against mixing up shared language elements). But if, say, you embark on Mandarin Chinese (a Sino-Tibetan language) and Russian (a Slavic language), like Matthias Maurer, you'll be subjected to a much greater challenge, just as you would if you decided to learn Arabic (a Semitic language) like Frank Gardner or Farsi (an Iranian language) like our diplomat Josh. Your task would be an even taller order if you plan to become literate in the respective scripts – Hanzi, Cyrillic and Arabic – too. But even then it's possible to engage some of the same learning strategies you've already developed: there is a fundamental logic in languages that is transferable when learning.

Building your language repertoire

We've already discussed the value of languages to our lives from multiple perspectives in this book. Among the long-term benefits are potentially enhanced cognitive function and the ability to engage as global citizens in a world of rapid change, which also gives rise to better job prospects.

We've seen too that, for many, learning a second language is just the start of a lifelong journey. Martina Navratilova, for example, says she is still as interested in other languages now as she was in her school days. With her ear for music, she's naturally attuned to new sounds in different language environments. She realizes that what helps her most is learning by listening and hearing, so she has developed her own technique to get by casually outside the langauges she's already familiar with. She readily picks up new languages once she understands how they work, and she's planning to learn Spanish next, because it's spoken in the Miami neighbourhood where she lives.

Like Martina, Matthias, Josh and many of the other multilingual characters we have encountered in this book, all of us are capable of continually expanding our repertoire of languages over our lifetimes. We can almost accidentally accumulate snippets of different languages through travel, new media and technology, all of which make languages more readily available. And as owners of mobile devices that offer on-the-spot assistance, constant progression has become easier for (would-be) users of many languages, at any stage of life.

Using languages all our lives

Lifelong learners continually build on their cognitive resources. In doing so they develop resilience: a multifaceted capacity to stay in control of their lives. Accumulating different skills to face challenges and to respond to them appropriately – whether through communication or otherwise – they're able to draw on all their internal resources, including the languages they have learned.

As we saw in Chapter 3, learning and using languages is one way of keeping your brain fit well into old age. The Healthy Linguistic Diet initiative proposes that:[94]

Regular physical activity and a healthy diet are important factors in maintaining physical health. In the same way, the learning of languages and their regular use provide essential mental exercise, leading to a better brain health and an increase in 'cognitive reserve' resulting in a later onset of dementia and an improved cognitive outcome after a stroke.

What is thought to happen is that, as parts of the brain succumb to (inevitable) decline, bilinguals are more able to compensate for cerebral loss. This is because, as we saw in Chapter 3, they have developed extra grey matter and alternative neural pathways.[95] The idea that languages are good for your health has generated some innovative social projects that use them as a mental stimulus for the elderly (we shall return to this in Chapter 7).

It is never too late to learn another language. In fact, tackling a new language does not get harder as we age: it is just different. Adults and children certainly acquire languages in their own ways: children absorb them organically and instinctively; adults focus on them more systematically. But there is no cut-off age after which a healthy adult cannot learn another language.[96]

Considering your learning architecture

This chapter has focused attention on you as a learner, asking what type of a person you are and what drives you in life. It has adopted a holistic perspective about *how* you learn, concerning itself less with the *technicalities* of that learning. Your route into languages can take many different forms, and it depends on the resources available to you and also on your previous experiences with languages.

As is the case with learning any new skill, acquiring the fundamentals is best achieved by a concentrated burst of study at the start of the process. The early stages of learning should help you gain an understanding of the way a particular language works and how you use it. Creative platforms that encourage playful repetition support the process of language acquisition, whether you're at the beginner stage or are more advanced, but as we have seen, they are likely to work better in combination with careful and deliberate practice. It's the same as learning to play the piano or ride a bike: repetition builds proficiency.

Once you've embedded the building blocks of a language you can start to branch out by immersing yourself in the language, as the various people we've met in this book have done. You'll have gathered from their real-life stories that different people have different language needs depending on their personal interests: a chef's requirements are different from those of a writer, an astronaut or a sportsperson. What they all have in common, though, is the same core, differing only at the periphery. In following their instincts they gradually started to branch out, applying their language skills to the context that was useful and relevant to them.

Overall, the progress we make when learning a language is less about the tools we choose and more about our methods, and the focus we apply. Online and offline study, apps and books all have their place – whether we are learning in an organized setting or an informal one – but how you choose to use the available resources depends both on their accessibility and on your particular objectives. Crucially, engaging more deeply with another language is an ongoing journey of development, interaction and discovery. If you are about to embark on this journey, you'll need to know about the opportunities that exist for you, and these are detailed in our next chapter.

CHAPTER 7

Where can I study languages?

BY NOW, I HOPE YOUR interest in studying languages has been kindled. You have read the 'why' arguments, but what about 'where'? In this chapter, we are going to take a look at the various choices that are available to you when it comes to your route into languages.

However much advice I give, though, some of the work has to be done by you: now is the time to think carefully about your choices so you can make an informed decision. To do this, you're going to have to think about what you want from the various stages of school and beyond. This doesn't mean you have to prepare a plan for your entire life now, though. It simply means that you need to choose your options while bearing in mind both what you want to do and – perhaps just as importantly – what you do *not* want to do at this point in your life.

Now is the time for you to take a stand and do what you love, rather than what you think you should do. In short, you have to take control of your learning and trust your intuition about the decision you're about to make. And in Britain's current educational climate, you'll face an additional hurdle: you'll need to ensure you have enough funding and know where to look for scholarships to make your dream choice happen.

I hope the advice below will be useful to you, no matter where you are on life's learning journey. The various educational phases I'm going to consider are school, university and college, and vocational and lifelong learning.[97]

Studying languages at school

If you enjoyed learning another language to age 16 (GCSE level in England, Wales and Northern Ireland, or National 5 in Scotland), there are many reasons for carrying on with languages in your last few years of school (e.g. doing an A level in the UK):

▶ You'll have the opportunity to further pursue a subject you are good at and develop a practical command of the language.

▶ It will be essential if you plan to study the language in question to degree level.

▶ Language is one of the 'facilitating' subjects at A level: that is, it is one of the subjects required by universities and colleges in entry requirements. So even if you aren't sure about continuing with language study after school, you may find that having a languages A level helps keep your options open.

Languages can be combined with any other A levels: mathematics, business studies, English literature, music, history, politics. I could go on. A language A level also keeps a wide range of degree options open to you, for a number of reasons. If you want to study a language at university that is not offered at school – and bear in mind that the options available to you after school are considerable – at least one A level in another language is normally required, or often preferred, as it shows that you have language-learning ability. So whatever language you might go on to study at university, at least one language A level should be in your line-up. Moreover, you can combine a language A level with other subjects at university: history with Spanish, for example, or geography and French, law and Italian, and so on.

Some things to think about at school

If my school offers it, should I study a language at GCSE and/or A level? If you're interested in studying a particular language at university, you'll need a language A level, but what A level will be required depends on the target language. If, like Josh (whom we met in Chapter 5), you were interested in Farsi, and you wanted to take it up at university, you almost certainly won't have an opportunity to take an A level in the language. Consequently, universities will instead require you to prove that you have language-learning ability through another A level language. If, on the other hand, you want to study German at university, then you should take it at A level if your school offers it.

If my school only offers one language choice, which one should I pick at university? My advice is: follow your feelings. If your school offers only French to A level, then it's still possible to study Russian at university if you want to. You will, though, need to convince the university of your dedication to the language (e.g. by visits to Moscow, online reading, family links) as well as doing well in your French A level.

How do I get into a good university to study languages? Ideally (but not necessarily), you need an A level in your target language. You should also try to build in extra experience in the language, so you can increase your confidence and strengthen your profile. You'll find that there are plenty of opportunities for doing so: look into volunteering in a place where the language is used; investigate the extra-curricular activities that your school offers; or think about completing a Real Lives challenge as part of your Duke of Edinburgh Award.[98]

At university, are there some languages that are a better bet to take up from beginners' level alongside one in which you are already competent? Most universities offer the option to start a new language as part of a combined or joint degree. And you can also carry on with a language you studied at school if you match the entry requirements. At the practical level, your choice of institution may well depend on which language, or combination of languages, you prefer. Perhaps you'd like to combine a global language with one that is spoken nearby: French and Italian, for example, for a native English speaker in the UK? Or maybe you'd prefer to study two global languages that are widely spoken on different continents: Chinese and Spanish, say. Your eventual success will depend on how well you match your skills with the opportunities that lie ahead; there is no 'ideal' language choice.

Should I take the opportunity to do a language module alongside my main subject at university? Many universities allow you to combine language study with another subject area, from economics to engineering, law to medicine. As was the case for Jacob, whom we met in Chapter 5, this will give you a complementary set of skills that future potential employers are likely to value. It might also open up opportunities in other countries that would not otherwise be available to you at home.

How can I fit in studying languages at university? If you don't want to opt for a specialist language degree, there should be numerous other options available to you at university that will allow you to combine language study with your main subject. These range from combined or joint degrees through to short units or modules (see below). The amount of time set aside for language study will vary depending on which option you pursue.

Studying languages at university

So you're faced with one of your biggest life decisions: what to study and where to study it. And there are other things you'll need to think about too: funding, for example, and whether to go on a gap year. These can be just as important as what you study, and they are a crucial part of you taking control of your learning.

Funding

You don't just have to pay for your food and accommodation at university, you also have to contribute towards the costs of the teaching you receive (i.e. fees). Until the late 1990s, going to university in the UK was free to students. The government paid the fees, with funds provided by the taxpayer, and the 7% of school leavers who attended university were given a grant. Nowadays, 50% of 18-year-olds go to university, and you have to pay for almost everything: all your food and accommodation and a fixed contribution towards your fees (the government pays the rest of the fees directly to the university).[99]

Several things flow from such changes to funding. Most importantly, you now need to find the resources needed to cover your education, as you will have to pay for some items up front before you can even begin your studies: a deposit for student accommodation and a term's worth of fees is a typical requirement. The sources of funding that are available are few: you can take out a student loan, you can enlist the support of your parents (or grandparents), you can do part-time work or take a gap year to earn some cash, or you can borrow money from a bank. If you're lucky, you might get sponsored by an organization (e.g. the military) or, sometimes, a company. Finally, some universities offer bursaries (more information on this is given in this book's appendix).

The vast majority of British students that attend a UK university take out a student loan: that is, they borrow money from the government and pay it back over the course of their working lives (subject to certain conditions). The student loan will be enough to cover your contribution to the fees, but it comes with a sting in the tail: the amount you get depends on how much your parents earn. If they earn a lot, you get less, with the idea being that they give you whatever else you need. But what if they can't, or won't?

If there's a shortfall, you'll need to consider earning some money or borrowing it from a bank. Don't be tempted to think you can work while you're at university, as very few students manage this effectively. Not only will you be one of many chasing the same limited number of on-campus jobs, but the time spent working will be time away from your studies – time that can't be regained later. Taking out a bank loan isn't really recommended either: the interest rates tend to be high, and you may have to repay the loan quicker than you're able to. You could try and save on your expenses by living at home with your family and commuting to a nearby university, as is the custom in many other countries, but this could mean missing out on the full university experience.

If your parents are able and willing to meet the costs of your time at university, you will have few worries, although you may need to be careful to ensure you study what you're really interested in rather than what your (paying) parents want you to do. Sadly, though, it is a significant source of stress to a large number of students when their parents cannot support them. Distant or absent parents are an obvious problem, and not one that the student loan scheme takes into account.

Gap year

Are you ready to go to university? Having lived at home until now, the prospect of going away to some possibly distant town or city to study might seem overwhelming. Maybe you need a break before you dive in, to give you extra confidence? Or perhaps you worked so hard in sixth form that you simply need some time off, to avoid burnout? Alternatively, you might be interested in doing some volunteering or seizing the chance to visit relatives overseas to shore up your language skills? Or maybe your longer-term plan involves moving straight into employment after university, so you think you should travel the world now, while you still can? All of these options are perfectly sensible reasons for taking a gap year. Only you will know what is best for you, so follow your instincts.

One of the arguments used for *not* taking a gap year is that you will forget everything you learned at school and find yourself at a disadvantage when you start studying a year later, but the reality is that even students who don't take a gap year will end up failing to remember a lot of their A level material. The gap year may turn out to be an intensely formative time in your life, teaching you valuable life skills as well as opening up doors to future opportunities. The extra life experience and the resilience you are likely to gain will help you navigate the turbulent waters of higher education. University tutors can always tell a gap year student by their greater confidence and maturity.

'Going to uni'

'Going to uni' has become a rite of passage for many young people. It is an opportunity to fill the time between being at school and having a job. But you need to be aware that not all universities are the same. What is more, universities are not simply big schools.

What is different at university, then? Since this is a book about language, let's first discuss the deep meaning of the word 'educate'. It comes from the Latin word *educare*, meaning *to lead out*. But who is doing the leading? It is, of course, your professors and tutors. Fortunately, they aren't robots, all programmed to see the world in the same way and to pass on their knowledge to you in a pre-packaged, YouTube-like way. It's natural that they will share some common traits (perhaps when teaching the structure of a language), but when it comes to cultural issues, one lecturer whose interest is the culture of German graffiti is not going to give the same advanced lectures as someone whose work focuses on how infants acquire languages in a bilingual household.

It's certainly true that you are the one being led, and that also implies agency on your part. You have to want to be led: 'you can lead a horse to water, but you can't make it drink', as the saying goes. This applies at school too, but there you had to attend for most of your education, because that's the law. If you played truant at school or did badly in class, the school would take action. By contrast, no one is forcing you to go to university, and all the responsibility falls on you. Now you need to organize your time and be self-disciplined about working and meeting deadlines, as well as looking after your work–life balance.

One final point before we start thinking about the specifics of studing languages at university. Just because someone is paying doesn't mean they decide what you should study. Going to university is not a straightforward financial transaction, like buying a car or a new pair of trainers. You don't buy your degree. Instead you are paying for the privilege of being exposed to high-level teaching in your chosen subject. What you make of that opportunity is your decision. 'Going to uni' might be the only chance you'll have in your life to focus exclusively and intensively on something you love, being given the luxury of an extended period of time to study it and to experience the rich rewards that come from being 'led out'.

Which university?

During the final year of your secondary education you'll be given the predicted grades that your school will submit with your university application form. So how do you decide which universities to apply to?

Around half of UK university students move away from home to go to university. If this feels like the best option for you too, how do you go about choosing which instutition is a good fit for you? Some students will want to try to get into Oxford or Cambridge, which have prestige and history that goes back centuries. Others will insist they have to end up in London. It is one of the most culturally diverse cities in the world and is home to almost every type of university. Maybe you want to be close to mountains or the sea, perhaps because you have a passion for climbing or sailing. Or perhaps a crucial factor for you will be wanting to live in the cocooned comfort of a campus, rather than being in a city. For others, though, the thrill of mixing with 'real people' in a city, as they move between university buildings, is an important sanity check.

Just by listing the various outlooks in the paragraph above, one can see that every student is different. Each knows what is important to them. Using the Uni Guide website (www.theuniguide.co.uk), you can filter your online choices by mode of study (e.g. full time or part time), your preferred place of study (maybe you really want to end up in a certain city, say), the type of course you want to take (one with a year abroad, perhaps, or maybe one with a sandwich option), the type of university (campus versus city, etc.), or how a university's students have rated it (for social life, student activities and so on).

We also see that one of the most important reasons listed by prospective applicants for favouring one university over another is that they identify with the current students, and with the ones they meet on Open Days. When choosing a university, then, make sure you go there before you apply, to see what the place and the people are like. Many universities will make it possible for you to chat with enrolled students, so make sure you have questions ready that are important to you. Try to talk to the other people on the tour as well: you may be studying with them soon after all.

The range of possible universities available to you will naturally be much narrower if you opt to live with your parents during your studies. In this case, you'll need to make sure your commuting distance is realistic and your daily travel costs are within your available budget.

Ways to study languages at university

There are many different ways to study languages at university, and not all of them are reflected in the degree titles you'll find. In general, you can enrol for either one language on its own, or as part of a joint degree course (with either another language or another subject), or as an option in another degree course. Some of these options, but not all of them, involve a year abroad.

Let's take the case of German. If you want to study only German, you would typically choose a four-year degree with one of the years being spent in a German-speaking country (at a university or on an internship, or both). When it comes to joint degree courses, you have to be very careful of the words 'and' and 'with'. If the degree course is called, say, 'German and history', you can usually expect approximately half of your time to be spent on German (in the languages department) and half on history (in the history department; note that you won't necessarily be restricted to German history). The degree will probably be administered by the languages department. On the other hand, the content of a 'German with history' degree might be three-quarters German and a quarter history (what is more, it's possible that you could choose a straight German degree and still take a few history options if you wanted to).

Suppose, instead, that you have set you heart on business studies but also prize the benefits of learning French. Your search finds courses such as 'International business *with* French (with a year abroad)' or 'French *and* business studies' (pay particular attention to the two words in italics here). Or maybe you'll choose business studies on its own and simply add a few optional language units as you go along (you'll need to check first to see if such choices are possible).

For STEM subjects and for vocational subjects like medicine and law, the combinations with languages are not as extensive as they are with other subjects. One sees more of the 'with' options than the 'and' ones, reflecting the demands of professional bodies that graduates can enter certain professions with only a small amount of non-core content. And yet a huge range of options is still available. You could study 'Engineering with a year abroad', for example (usually a four-year degree). In your first two years, your engineering timetable would probably contain a dedicated language unit (e.g. 'German for scientists and engineers'), and then you might spend your third year in a German-speaking country, returning to complete your final year at your home university. Note, too, that you may not need to have studied your chosen language at school (this is especially true if you opt for languages not normally taught at school, such as Mandarin).

One language on its own, or as part of a joint degree course?

If you are deciding between studying one language on its own or pursuing it as part of a joint degree course, you'll need to make sure your school-leaving grades in that language match the stated admission prerequisites. Universities vary widely in terms of the A level language requirements for their degree courses. Some will ask for an A grade in your main language (and possibly a B in any additional language you might want to study). And then there are universities where you may get a place with a B grade, or a C, or two Es. Some even make unconditional offers.

Certain universities use the UCAS tariff points system, which converts your exam grades into points. Bear in mind that different language degrees will have different entry requirements, so be sure to check the conditions for specific courses before you finalize your choices if you want to keep your degree options open. Search the Uni Guide site to see what the requirements are, to help you choose where to study, and to investigate which possible combinations suit you. You can also find out more details about what is involved and the entry routes for Scottish Highers students on the UCAS languages search tool. Moreover, your school or college should be able to assist you with your university choices and applications in Year 12 or Year 13.

Universities also vary widely when it comes to the range of languages and the combinations of subjects they offer, so you'll need to make sure your preference is available where you're hoping to enrol.

If we go back to our previous example and assume that you always wanted to study Farsi after school, there are few universities that offer this rare choice. Oxford has ten different four-year language courses, with most students having studied French at school. By contrast, the University of St Andrews currently offers 124 options (not all of which have a year abroad), with tuition fees set significantly lower if you happen to live in Scotland.

Both modern and ancient language degrees will selectively include the history, literature, culture and politics of the language, as well as some translation and linguistics (the science behind language and communication). Some universities may also offer a subject specialism: German language and culture in Austria, say, or you might focus on one of the regional language communities in Spain (Galician, Catalonian, Basque).

Language degrees are taught in specialist departments that might carry the name of their language (e.g. the Department of Russian). You'll frequently find these language departments grouped together in larger units, under names such as modern languages, languages and cultures, or languages and area studies. You should be able to retrieve information on the languages offered from those departments, as well as tracking down timetables and enrolment options. Department websites will also give you a flavour of the areas of research being pursued by their staff and their postgraduate students: anything from identity to gender, linguistics to politics, migration to literary studies. These special interests may inform some of the units being offered as part of the various courses.

At the end of your course, you'll earn a degree that reflects the length of time you spent studying and where you spent that time. So you'll obtain a BA (Hons), a Bachelor's degree, if you studied full time for three years in an arts faculty to a high ('honours') level. Or, if you decide to carry on with your studies for one or, more commonly, two extra years, you'll receive an MA (Hons): a Master's level award.

Studying a language as an option in another degree course

In all universities it's also possible to combine a language with another subject. Just like the students we met in Chapter 1, you can take a language module whether you are based in the arts (e.g. history, philosophy, art and design), the social sciences (e.g. economics, law, sociology) or the natural sciences (e.g. biology, physics, geography). Science, technology, engineering and mathematics (STEM) degrees can also come with a credited language component.

You should be aware that certain courses – international studies, for instance, or marketing, or business communication – may not make specific reference to the particular languages that are taught alongside them. It is worth your while paying close attention to the actual course details: even courses that have identical titles can vary between institutions. You should also be able to find out more details about the language component offered, e.g. what percentage of the overall course it makes up.

For combined degrees with a language component – that is, either a technical subject or a social or natural science plus a language – you will find many different possible options, depending on your previous language experience. You'll often be required to have a minimum of a GCSE in the relevant language, to enable you to study or work abroad in a country where that language is used as part of your third year. The content of the language unit will tend to relate to your core subject, whether it be physics, chemistry, engineering or economics. These four-year degree courses often have a name such as 'Engineering with study abroad'; with an MEng in mechanical engineering with German, say, you could earn yourself a highly employable qualification.

Elective language modules

If you're not up to the appropriate language level to pursue a particular subject at the postgraduate level (English literature, perhaps, or classics), you can attend a language unit. Many universities have a language centre (or similar) where you can take extra modules. These can be in a specific language (e.g. Mandarin, Korean, Arabic, British sign language, etc.) or non-language module (e.g. on the history and culture of a language), and they can count towards your degree result.

Moreover, if that's too much of a commitment, or if you want to learn a new language from scratch, you could join an evening class run by the university, which are also often open to the general public. Alternatively, you may prefer to work independently in a self-access unit, where you can draw on books and accompanying audio as resources, as well as TV channels from the country of your chosen language.

These modules and classes are available to all students who wish to develop their language skills at various levels of proficiency, from beginner to advanced. With this great diversity and flexibility of courses on offer you should easily be able to find a language option that is a good fit for you.

Learning, teaching and assessment

As you'll have gathered by now, your time at university is organized quite differently from school. In fact, a lot of it will not be organized for you at all. You are in control of your learning to a much greater extent than before, giving you plenty of time for independent study. The new styles of teaching that you'll experience and the time-management skills that you develop will be invaluable to you beyond university. In addition, you'll develop a wide range of communicative, practical and interpersonal skills, all of which are transferable into your future career.

Another big difference at university is the way in which your work is assessed. Sure, there are the obligatory written exams and interim tests, and your essays will be marked. But how you interact within a group may also be assessed, as might your presentational skills. What is more, in some teamwork exercises, the contribution of each participating member could be graded by the other members of the group and not by the lecturer. In choosing a suitable course of study, you will therefore also need to investigate how the teaching works and how you will be assessed. This is all part of the same message: not all universities are the same. You need to think about what works best for you, given your current strengths. For example, do you like sitting and listening to a teacher, or do you prefer private study?

You should also take into account areas of potential development for the future. If you've ever done any acting, say, maybe you'll turn out to be good at presentations. Employers value such 'soft skills', and all universities now assess them in some part of each programme. Immersing yourself in an extended project can therefore be a good way to work independently and demonstrate your research skills, and your effective communication of complex ideas in the language you are studying.

Learning

The fact that you are in charge of your learning at university cannot be overemphasised. But what does it actually mean?

Well, it all starts the moment you begin to think about what to study. You already made one big step by buying this book! Talking to friends, relatives and schoolteachers, and researching and reading information online are all part of that process of you taking charge.

Academically speaking, you'll be going to university to acquire knowledge, understanding and a whole range of skills. But acquiring knowledge is not the same as just remembering things, and this is probably the single biggest difference between school and university. You will certainly have to absorb and retain new information at first. But true learning only comes with time and immersion and persistence and joy and agency. The in-depth language experience you'll gain during your study abroad is similar to the process of practising, and then knowing, how to ride a bicycle: eventually you'll be able to express your ideas without searching for words or struggling with the structure of the language – even without consciously doing any translating.

Your marks, then, are now secondary, as they will flow from the deep knowledge you gain. While at school, success is often related to the grades you obtain, not least because schools are under enormous pressure to achieve better results. The upshot of this is that 'what is not counted does not count'. This results in many students focusing chiefly on marks that count towards their final scores, meaning that they'll miss out on other, equally important aspects of learning and forget much of what they have learned as a result.

At university, by contrast, and as in real life, some things really matter even if you get no marks for them: that formative essay that you didn't bother finishing may be there to help with a summative assessment. It is these deeper aspects of learning that you ought to focus on at university. You need to develop an understanding that learning is a journey: from not knowing to knowing. Remembering is only the first stop on your life-long quest to knowing.

Teaching
Make sure you find out what proportion of your studies is given over to language learning. As an undergraduate you'll be focused on improving your competence in your target language as well as studying aspects of the societies and cultures associated with it. You'll be offered plenty of opportunities to learn through the medium of the language you are studying, although not all instruction is necessarily delivered in that language. Remember that language learning at all levels is intensive in terms of both teaching contact and independent study, and you'll be encouraged to carry out

regular and extended practice in the language, using various offline and online resources.

For degrees where you take the language as an option, the course content and the language skills you'll be practising are often tailored to the specific purposes of your studies. Working with materials that are tailored to your core discipline will help you develop the tools you need for understanding key concepts, for problem solving and for communicating about your subject matter more effectively with others. It will also prepare you for your period abroad, during which you might be asked to write a subject-specific project in the target language. On your return to your home university, you'll often have an opportunity to consolidate your acquired skills and knowledge.

The teaching methods you encounter will vary depending on the overall aims and objectives of your degree course. In all cases, you'll be exposed to authentic materials in your target language as early as possible. This will include digital and print media to improve your reading and listening comprehension. You'll also be given tasks that develop your ability to use and present material in the language. You may have to give oral presentations or actively participate in guided discussions and debates, as well as completing essays and extended projects on which you'll receive feedback. You can expect some teaching of grammar, often assisted by IT resources, perhaps in addition to some targeted translation work from and into your primary language.

Assessment

Universities vary hugely not only in terms of their teaching but also when it comes to their assessment methods. Depending on the objectives of the course, more focus may be placed on assessing your knowledge of the target language itself, or on your understanding of its associated culture and society. You'll also be given a range of tests for demonstrating your passive (reading/listening) and active (written/oral) proficiency in the language, and you will have opportunities to independently develop your research skills and techniques for collecting and selecting your material for interaction and presentation. There will also be opportunities for your own self-assessment to check on your progression.

Language graduates normally reach a high level of understanding in their target language. Among the many skills that are assessed at this level are also subject-related ones: that is, your critical understanding of the cultures, communities and societies in which the studied language is used, and possibly also your knowledge of the country or region itself. Since different language departments will vary when it comes to the weight they place on your understanding of these elements, their method of assessing your achievements will vary too.

Students who choose an elective language unit can also earn credits based on attendance, completing essential homework, and a final exam that tests proficiency in the target language. This is usually assessed in relation to the Common European Framework of Reference for Languages (CEFR), and a final unit mark is given.

Language proficiency

Language proficiency is understood as a set of skills that can be measured according to international standards. The CEFR has a system for defining your language ability at various stages of mastery: from beginner through intermediate to advanced.[100] Three components of proficiency are assessed: content (the range of topics you can communicate about), function (the type of spoken or written tasks you're able to carry out) and accuracy (the correctness of your use of the target language).

An assessment grid is used to categorize what a student should be able to do in listening, speaking, reading and writing at three pairs of language levels, ranging from 'basic' (A1/2) to 'intermediate' (B1/2) and then 'proficient' (C1/2). For example, in speaking, a learner at the basic level is expected to demonstrate an ability to exchange simple information (e.g. asking questions about a menu), someone at the intermediate level should have a capacity to deal with more general information (e.g. opening a bank account), and at the proficient level, one should be able to demonstrate the faculty to process cognitively demanding information to good effect (e.g. discussing the pros and cons of migration).

The CEFR scheme that measures your proficiency in a target language makes it possible to give differentiated descriptions of your language skills, which may be required if you apply for a job or university place abroad. You can also use it for self-assessment by filling in checklists of 'I can' descriptors: things like 'I can write a short, simple postcard, for example sending holiday greetings' (A1 basic user/writing); or 'I can understand extended speech and lectures ... [and] most current affairs programmes' (B2 independent user/ listening). In adopting an action-oriented approach, proficiency is measured here as a set of competencies that varies from individual to individual in terms of extent and depth of use. As such, this type of assessment usefully complements the pliable term 'fluency' or the vague notion of 'knowing a language'.

A study period abroad

Many degrees with a large language component encourage students to spend some time in a country where the language is spoken (often in the third year of a four-year course). This period abroad can encompass study or a work placement (an internship), and it is set to be supported by the new UK-funded Turing scheme.[101] For those unable to spend an extended period living abroad, a variety of alternative options are often made available, such as directed intensive language study during vacations or contact with the target language environment through digital resources and/or 'virtual mobility' schemes.

You'll find this part of your course incredibly valuable, as it makes a significant contribution to the development and enhancement of your knowledge, your understanding and your skills in both the language and related studies. In addition, your time abroad will promote your intercultural awareness and capabilities, as well as helping you develop self-reliance and other transferable skills. Think back to the students we met in Chapter 1: they all saw their year spent abroad as a formative phase of their education.

You'll also find that universities vary in how they expect students to make use of their period abroad, what tasks they're asked to carry out, the ways in which their activities are supported, monitored and assessed, and the means by which this part of their learning is integrated into the overall course objectives. Make sure you understand exactly what is expected of you, then, as you will certainly encounter different styles of teaching depending on the culture you become embedded in, and student life will be different as well.

Perhaps you're wondering whether being far away from home for a long stretch of time will mean you'll have to move out of your comfort zone? Or maybe you're asking yourself whether you can handle a university experience that is very different from the one you're used to? The good news is that universities that engage in student exchanges will have a range of staff on board whose job it is to look after people like you. Moreover, you'll be able to rely on continuing long-distance support from your home institution too.

During your stay abroad you may not always be aware that you are learning, but you will continually be improving by absorbing new aspects of the language and culture, by listening, watching and trying out different ways of saying things. To achieve steady progression, though, you'll also need to bring some structure into your learning to help your brain retain the ongoing stimulus it is receiving. For this reason it will be crucial that you develop and reflect on your own language-learning techniques, in order to deepen your freshly absorbed knowledge. This is a time when you really do need to take charge of your approach.

The opportunity to study or work abroad as part of your third year also facilitates a vocationally oriented experience for STEM students. Our astronaut, Matthias Maurer, found spending his third undergraduate year studying material science at the University of Leeds to be

> *the best investment I've made: being in a different country, learning material science at an excellent level, and at the same time also learning a language and being immersed in that environment, I was so motivated.*[102]

Like Matthias, many returners find that their time abroad gives them an advantage when they begin their careers. Once you've become proficient with the language used in your field of work, you're poised to become a bilingual professional – something that is a sought-after asset to employers, as we saw with Jacob Gilbert in Chapter 5 (see page 91).

Applying to university

Once you've made up your mind about which course at which particular university in the UK is a good fit for you, you need to apply online through the central Universities and Colleges Admissions Service (UCAS). Since competition for some places is intense, you're advised to find ways of making your application stand out. If possible, try to enlist help from someone who knows you academically. Ask them to talk about how you've developed your skills and experience, how you work and interact with other students, and why you are suitable for a particular degree course. You also need to submit a personal statement, so ensure that this reflects your interest in – and experience with – languages. This will greatly help your application as decisions are not based on grades alone. Universities will then assess your application and decide whether or not to offer you a place.

Institutions vary hugely when it comes to admission requirements. If, for example, you're applying for a pure language degree, you may be asked to demonstrate your fluency by completing a written test in the target language. Universities will also be looking for evidence that you're interested in, and well informed about, the language and related culture, and that you have the motivation required. This could be demonstrated by relevant work experience and/or travel in countries where your target language is spoken, or through participation in an exchange programme. Alternatively, evidence of additional reading and research, listening to the radio or watching films from different countries, and membership of language clubs are all valued signposts. Your range of interests outside of academic study will also be examined, as will your ability to work individually and as part of a team. Institutions will also want to see that you have the personal qualities required for successful study. Be sure you submit a persuasive statement that demonstrates your ability in the language as well as conveying your interests, strengths, motives and aspirations.

Alternative pathways

For vocational study, there is always the possibility for placements, internships and apprenticeships abroad. In countries where the Erasmus⁺ scheme is not supported, any such arrangements will have to be done on an ad hoc basis, and they are likely to require some proof of language ability.

Other opportunities for language study abroad are offered by various national institutions: the Instituto Cervantes for Spanish, the Alliance Française for French, the Foundation for Japanese, and the Confucius Institute for Chinese, for example. The purpose of these organizations is to foster international cultural exchange and relations through the medium of the languages they promote. Additionally, numerous international language education agencies exist that offer networked opportunities for language experiences through internships, volunteering opportunities or recreational activities in various countries.

If this is not an avenue you want to go down, you may instead explore different pathways to your career on the UCAS website, where you can also find advice on getting a job and learn what skills employers are looking for.[103]

Language skills and employability

Naturally, the way we work nowadays is being affected by the period of rapid change we're living in. Jobs are increasingly done on the move, at different times of day, and in almost any location. Many career paths are no longer linear: people are more likely than ever before to switch jobs, to work for employers of varying sizes, and to set up their own businesses. The careers of the future will therefore require particular skills, qualities and aptitudes, and you will need to be adaptable, flexible, willing to upskill, and motivated to adjust to different work environments.

Not only is having a second language useful if you decide to study abroad as part of your degree, it can also improve your future employability. With skills in languages you can better position yourself in the domestic labour market as well as being able to apply for a much wider range of jobs in other countries. Employers will normally set out specific required skills, and these can include proficiency in another language if that's relevant to a project or work assignment they're planning.

Lots of employers who aren't looking for languages as their main focus are still interested in them as a valued extra. Many of them seek people with language skills because they know this helps them to adapt their business to different sets of international environments and to operate with greater cultural agility and insight. The key skills they are looking for include the following.

► Technical know-how (hard skills) as well as cultural aptitude (soft skills). Languages, here, are often seen as adding intellectual capital.

► Another highly valued quality is resilience: the ability to cope with setbacks and criticism, to be motivated to overcome obstacles, and to stay calm under pressure.

► A positive attitude to work, flexibility and verbal communication skills (which are often seen to be closely connected to language study) are among the top requirements on the job market.

All these skills are transferable, which means you can hone them in any learning, work or social setting and then use or enhance them in other contexts. Building on your personal toolkit in this way will help you become adaptable and flexible and be able to cope with change.

These abilities can often be further developed through vocational education and training, such as an apprenticeship or a foundation degree. Experiences of this type tend to be recognized by trade and professional bodies and may provide a licence to practise. What is more, you'll already be armed with a significant array of skills and knowledge. Perhaps you've also accumulated language experience through time spent abroad. With focus and imagination, you'll find a way of building your skillset into your work. The secret to success in life, as in the job market, is to deploy your strengths to your advantage.

Multinational organizations want multilingual recruits

The employment stories of the professionals we met in Chapter 5 showed that successful intercultural communication is seen as key in multinational organizations. In order to enhance their profit, many companies invest in different language support systems to improve the quality of their service provision, administration and infrastructure. A pragmatic and time-honoured approach for workplaces is to improve on-site communication by tapping into existing language resources and using the skills of bilingual staff. As well as bringing immediate results, this option is usually cost effective. Alternatively, employers may provide or facilitate language training for their personnel, e.g. by arranging a placement in one of a company's overseas subsidiaries.

On the other hand, where language skills are a requirement for a particular job, a basic proficiency will rarely be regarded as sufficient. In recruitment, the use of the term 'fluency' tends to imply a standard beyond higher education entrance level: here, an employee is normally expected to be able to perform work assignments in that language. Often this needs to be at an advanced or more specific business level. Employers know that an ability to confidently negotiate a wine import deal using French with the correct tone, say, is likely to pay dividends, since no amount of translation can be as effective or persuasive as face-to-face communication.

This is even more true in the stage before a contract is signed, when being able to interact effectively in the language of a trade partner really counts. Quite apart from understanding technical references, a joke, a pun or tiny nuances that may easily get lost in translation could eventually turn out to matter. However, while multilingual skills are important, they are by no means the only requirement in intercultural communication. Anyone who engages with people from a range of language backgrounds will need an awareness of how cultural differences can affect social relationships and outcomes. This is where soft skills come in.

It is beyond doubt that the ability to speak more than one language is an asset in a 'global economy', as is knowledge of different cultures. We can see why headhunters are eager to recruit people who have the cultural and language know-how to deal effectively with colleagues and clients abroad for work in a wide range of sectors. The key areas of employment in which languages are directly required or are useful include the civil service, education, hospitality and tourism, IT and telecommunications, law, marketing and publishing, media and journalism, recruitment and human resources, retail sales and customer service, transport and logistics. You can find more information about graduate destinations and alternative pathways – about internships or industrial placements, for example – on the UCAS website.

Professional qualifications and volunteering

This chapter would not be complete without a discussion of the vocational routes involving languages that may be open to you, at both the postgraduate and post-school levels. Whether you're a bilingual adult or simply enjoyed that real-life language challenge project at school (see above), it's never too late to consolidate your language skills. Doing so might even take you along a new work path in your life.

At the postgraduate level, you may earn yourself an internationally recognized Diploma in Translation, which gives you a professional qualification at the Master's level. This diploma entitles you to recognition for a career mediating for technology, business, social science or law in the competitive translation marketplace. Alternatively, you might opt for a degree-level Diploma in Public Service Interpreting, which could see you working in the areas of law, healthcare, local government or for the police.[104]

If you have a flair for languages, there are also routes that you could follow that would see you working with them straight after school. One such opportunity is offered through the Royal Air Force, which operates a scheme whereby you can receive technical and language training to become an intelligence analyst. The languages that they teach change depending on operational requirements, but at the time of writing you could find yourself studying Arabic, Russian and Farsi if you pursue this avenue. Getting to grips with any of these languages would, however, be a tall order for anyone who is accepted by this scheme with (the required minimum of) two GCSE grades and without any prior experience with languages. Still, you'll be given an opportunity to learn a language here while being paid on the job, but in return you'll have to commit to this organization for a number of years following your qualification.[105]

Another option, if you have a languages background of any type, is to get involved in volunteering. One possibility is working with elderly people to promote their life-long learning. Activities within the University of the Third Age have led to the emergence of pioneering social enterprises for those who want to get together with others who are interested in languages. A Scottish project called Yaketyyak has language cafes and bistros for people who would like to 'yak' with others in a relaxed atmosphere: in Spanish, Japanese or Irish, perhaps. Another scheme, Lingo Flamingo, caters for those recovering from brain injury, for the elderly and for those with dementia in care homes, using languages as a platform for stimulating their brains.

These initiatives were perhaps motivated by the evidence we've already seen about the use of languages keeping our brains fit well into old age. Possibly because people are now living longer and looking for some intellectual stimulation as they age, language learning is becoming an increasingly popular activity in later life, and particularly in retirement. Apart from the reported cognitive benefits that the use of languages brings, the strong social component also helps counteract feelings of isolation, thereby supporting overall well-being.

Last but not least

You can study languages for many different reasons: for love, for travel, or to give you greater opportunities. And there's no downside to learning another language either. Everything depends on what sort of a person you want to be, so when answering the question posed by this book's title, you really need to be thinking about what you want to do with your life.

Languages help you understand different cultures, and they enable different ways of thinking and doing things. They are one of the keys to knowledge, and they allow you to adapt to change and become more resilient. Languages are what you need in order to read, understand and debate the key issues that affect us all every day.

The demand for language skills is ever present, both in the UK and abroad. A language gap is particularly prominent in the labour market. Language skills have been found to contribute up to 10% of a country's GDP, and for you personally, your skills in languages will offer a real advantage when it comes to employment, enhancing your career opportunities both at home and overseas.

Languages give you an edge: an essential tool to thrive as a global citizen in a rapidly changing world. They allow you to make a difference and they mean you won't be left out of the conversation. Study what you love, and you'll do well. You're bound to find a way to build languages into your life and work. Believe in yourself and enjoy your learning journey.

POSTSCRIPT

A personal language journey

A FEW YEARS AGO, MY husband and I spent our sabbatical leave in Denmark. I wasn't planning to learn Danish for my stay there: I had other things lined up to do! And anyway, colleagues and neighbours back in Bristol would say prior to my departure: 'Don't worry, they can all speak English really well.' And indeed, many of them can, but that doesn't necessarily mean we always want to use English as a first resort when we're abroad. As a native of Switzerland, I had a diverse range of languages to draw on in order to interact with people in Denmark, including German, which is related to Danish. As it was, though, things turned out quite differently to how I imagined. Below you'll find extracts from my personal notebook entries on my language life while in Copenhagen, pretty much unedited from when I initially recorded them.

∽⁕∾

15 February

I find myself transiting into the Danish language quite unawares. When on our arrival the customs officer asks '*Vi reiser samme?*' (Are you travelling together?), my reply '*Ja, samme, tak!*' (Yes, together, thank you!) comes quite naturally. I must have absorbed these three words watching the (subtitled) Nordic Noir drama series *The Bridge* (*Broen*), and the fact that they are similar to German helped me remember them. To my surprise, the officer smiles encouragingly and lets us through. This easy first encounter in Danish with an actual Dane motivates me to read the notices and signs around. I soon spot big posters in the airport offering free Danish language courses. Why not take up this opportunity and push at a door that I find ajar already?

12 March

As it happens, I am enjoying my Danish course. I join a beginners' class run for immigrants and refugees. It is great to be a learner again and to engage my brain in new ways. With my native German, I find Danish straightforward to get into. So, I am enjoying an easy ride with my new language, initially. My classmates, mostly from Ethiopia, Iran and Syria, are facing a harder task to get going. Ismal, Reza, Hamel and Amira are working assiduously. They need to, because their own languages (Amharic, Arabic, Farsi and Kurdish) are quite distant to Danish. They must also learn to use the Latin script in order to read and write in Danish. I am in awe of their perseverance and zest to get going in a new place. They are so motivated and are progressing well. I soon find out that after class, they are busy working as casual labourers and writing job applications, which the language school (*Studieskolen*) offers to vet for them.

28 March

This course is entirely focused on the vocabulary and phrases newcomers need to know to find a job in the country. It uses an electronic textbook that's aptly entitled *Velkommen*. This material is presented in a way that enables instruction entirely in Danish. We learn basic phrases that are useful to us, starting with 'What are you called? Do you speak Danish?' (*Hvad hedder du? Taler du dansk?*). Our course material is supplemented with grammar notes, exercises and wordlists. The teaching is focused on repetition, and we gradually improve our basic language skills through practice. We are also expected to work at home. During the span of three months the complexity of what we can say gradually builds up. I am beginning to enjoy writing some simple Danish, too.

1 April

On today's visit to the Copenhagen public library, an innovative building in the shape of a huge black diamond (*en sort diamant*), I bump into Reza. Over coffee and cake (*kaffe og kage*) we share our stories, moving along the narrow confines of our freshly accumulated language fragments. I am fascinated by how much information we are able to exchange. A Kurdish refugee from Iran who works as an engineer, he had lost several members of his family in the political struggles. I sense how these memories are affecting him. Now he wants to make his living in the West. We share some information about things Danish and then part our ways.

2 April

Yesterday's encounter sets me on a path of reflection. In our classroom we are destined to do simple exercises that hardly reflect our inner selves. Learning this language is an act of survival for them; I have the luxury to do it for sheer pleasure. I shall never forget their strength and determination. By contrast, I can afford to follow my life-long instinct to connect with people on their own terms.

14 April

I find myself beginning to love this seemingly elusive language. The more I learn, the more I become eager to know. Every day, I find myself noting down on my mobile phone new words I come across (often I first need to check on their meanings as I go along, using online translation tools). I bring home free postcards picked up in town and post them on our fridge. They convey simple messages: *Smil når du sover* (Smile when you sleep) or *Tag det roligt* (Take it easy). These bite-size wisdoms pop up in my head as I go through the day.

Sometimes I draw big colourful posters that display the time of the day, things about the seasons, different ways of moving, bits of the city and parts of the body. I attach the posters around the high walls of our old attic apartment. Whenever I walk past them, I add new Danish words to the drawings. And I find myself counting a lot. Danish numbers are hard: the tens from fifty to ninety are based on the number 20 (not 10), the score. But the score is nowadays not mentioned in the number. So, for example 75 is *femoghalvfjerds*;

literally: five plus 4 scores minus half (a score) $(5 + (4 \times 20) - 10)$. I find myself becoming totally immersed in the necessary mental acrobatics required when counting, and I practise Danish numbers when chopping up carrots, telling the time of the day and turning the pages in the books I am reading.

16 April

Despite my imperfections with the language, my growing interest in all things Danish earns me much kindness. Shop assistants wait patiently before answering my simple, accented queries. I am able to chat to my hairdresser about the Eurovision song contest being held in the city later that year. When my local baker tells me how much I owe her she smiles benevolently as I try to figure out in my head how much to give her. I soon find out that the famous Danish pastry comes in many shapes and sizes and that locals call it *wienerbrød*, after a Viennese recipe.

I get to know the other regular bakery customers, too. One of them tells me that the vanilla cream filling in the middle of this pastry is meant to represent the original baker's once puss-filled eye (*fisse øje*, I had to look that up). Naturally perhaps, I become interested in other types of equally delicious treats, the *kanelstang, frøsnapper* and *hindbærsnitter*. And I find myself more confident when making choices and ready to enquire about the type of rye bread (*rugbrød*) on offer. These encounters are a highlight of my morning.

22 April

I am intrigued about this language and happy to keep up my efforts to connect with its speakers and their culture. I learn about the Danish sense of community and responsibility (*janteloven*), the legacy of Grundtvig and Kierkegaard, the imaginative work of filmmakers, designers and musicians. All these facets of culture matter to me because they matter to my temporary hosts.

25 April

My adventure with Danish has now lasted two months, and I am beginning to develop a feel for the language. It comes across to me as soft yet at times pointed, perhaps also a little monotonous. Yet the numerous Danish vowels can be difficult to pronounce. And then there are those blurred word endings and glottal stops to stumble over, all pronounced at breakneck speed.

In today's reflections about the Danish language and culture, I happen to come up with a style metaphor: Danes are well known for their hallmark sleek, streamlined design. Could the practised minimalism be inspired by a mindset that has also stripped the language to its bare essentials? Such as favouring sliding vowels to gloss over backstage consonants. The 'soft D' is a case in point: to me, it sounds like an 'L'. Or is it a different sound altogether? The oral acrobatics needed to perfect the drill are certainly most intriguing and for me, I know, completely out of reach. This manner of speaking requires a level of inner softness that feels not unlike a stylish Jacobsen chair, curving innovatively around the body of its occupant for new levels of comfort.

28 April

Today my stay has taken a surprising turn. The ice has finally melted in the city's canals, and so I decide to cycle down to the local rowing club. I have never rowed before, but the presence of water all round the city spurs my interest in this activity. I check out the key words I need to know to make this specific contact.

Once in the wharf, I pick up courage and talk to two fit looking elderly women, Merete and Åase. Is the club open to newcomers? Do they accept a novice? I find them a bit hesitant at first. They explain that Danish is the sole language spoken in the club, and that the teams use specific rowing commands. Am I up for it? They agree to a trial outing with me, but only once I have mastered the key Danish rowing instructions that they would email me. Also, I must practise the rowing strokes in the boathouse tank beforehand.

10 May

Today is my first rowing outing. I am looking forward to the adventure, not without some trepidation. My two friendly instructors are calm. They take me to a fine wooden longboat anchored for our tour and explain how to step in, fix the oar, settle down on my sliding seat, fasten my feet. I follow their steady strokes. Their voices are clear, the water is smooth, the weather benign. Halfway we slow down, we rest, and I learn to turn around the boat. I find myself expanding with the language into new territory in tandem with my oar in hand. They are satisfied with my physical (and oral) performance and invite me to join them again.

28 May

With my life shifting to the waterside, my relationship with people around me is changing, too. Rowing brings me closer to my fellow oars(wo)men, who gradually adopt me as one of theirs. In the team I learn how to load, handle, navigate, anchor, clean and store a different boat each time. I find my vocabulary growing in many different directions for ready export into my offshore life.

I become familiar with how to describe the weather conditions, the state of the water and rowing techniques. I follow directions on how to row through narrow canal tunnels and learn to steel my wave-averse nerves. With my mind and body fully immersed in these activities, I notice how my Danish is becoming easier, more intuitive. This change is almost visceral. I am actually beginning to *feel* the words I am using, the phrases I am saying. They express what I am, see and hear at that time. I am, I think, beginning to feel at home in the language.

4 June

In time I want to share my impressions in Danish and write this text for my class:

> *Tre gange om ugen ror jeg med Københavns Roklub. Roning er en fantastisk aktivitet. Vi ror fra Trømmelgade gennem smukke kanaeler til Langelinie. Når vejret er godt, sejler vi ud til Trekroner. Her deler vi frugt og kaffe. Disse ture er altid et dejligt eventyr. Selvfølgelig snakker vi alle Dansk til roning: dette er min bedste Dansk undervisning, og det er meget sjovt!*

This translates as:

> *Three times per week I row in the Copenhagen Rowing Club. Rowing is a great exercise. We row from [the Boathouse in] Trømmelgade through beautiful canals to [the landing place at] Langelinie. When the weather is good, we sail out to the Trekroner [island]. Here we share some fruit and coffee. These tours are always a great adventure. We all talk Danish of course when rowing: this is my best Danish lesson and it is great fun!*

12 September (eve of return to Bristol)

Summer has gone by, and Danish is feeling more embedded. This language journey hasn't been effortless but was well worth it. Now, visibly shorter days are heralding our departure. Rereading these entries gives me a warm glow. During this stay my horizon widened, both physically and mentally. I look forward to returning to Denmark.

✍

Rowing with Danes has given me new and lasting friendships. I am warmly welcomed back at the club on my annual returns to the city.

I feel fortunate to have consolidated my relationship with the rowers and, in reactivating my Danish, my connection with the society.

All this is way more than I'd bargained for when I first came to Denmark. Completely immersing myself in the language and culture opened up a new world for me, and it has changed me, too. The experience was both reinvigorating and rejuvenating. It refreshed my sense of adventure, the joy of learning new skills and the pleasures of being active in a diverse world.

APPENDIX

Finding out more

THIS APPENDIX SERVES AS A rough guide to various language initiatives and organizations that might prove helpful to you. You'll also find references to blogs and news sites, which will give you more of a feeling for the excitement of learning and knowing languages. More links to resources can be found in the endnotes. All URLs are correct as of 9 January 2021.

Why study languages?

▶ '700 reasons for studying languages' (2005). An online resource bank with collected research-based materials on studying languages: www.llas.ac.uk/publications/6034.html.

▶ 'Lead with languages' promotes language learning at all levels of education through stories, news and views: www.leadwithlanguages.org/why-learn-languages/top-ten-reasons-to-learn-languages/.

▶ The 'Speak to the future' initiative makes the case for language skills in Britain. It provides information and support about language learning and professional language activities across the UK: www.speaktothefuture.org/.

Information about studying languages in higher education
The links below provide information about the study of languages in universities.

▶ UCAS Languages: www.ucas.com/explore/subjects/languages.

▶ TheUniGuide: www.theuniguide.co.uk/advice/a-level-choices/what-a-levels-do-you-need-to-study-a-modern-language.

▶ Turing scheme (replacing Erasmus+): www.gov.uk/government/news/new-turing-scheme-to-support-thousands-of-students-to-study-and-work-abroad

- ▶ Scholarships for Languages: www.thescholarshiphub.org.uk/ scholarships-foreign-languages/.

Language learning experiences

- ▶ 'The case for language learning': www.theguardian.com/ education/series/the-case-for-language-learning.
- ▶ 'How learning a foreign language changed my life': www.bbc.co.uk/news/uk-47390760 (*BBC News*, 27 February 2019).
- ▶ 'Language graduates: what jobs are they doing now?': www.theguardian.com/education/2013/oct/16/ language-graduates-jobs (Lu-Hai Liang, *The Guardian*, 16 October 2013).
- ▶ Job profiles on the website of Scotland's National Centre for Languages (SCILT): https://scilt.org.uk/Portals/24/ Library/Leaflets/Job%20Profiles%20-%20booklet.pdf.

Language learning activities

However you learn languages, and whenever you do so, it's always possible to supplement your studies with extra-curricular language activities, some examples of which are listed below.

- ▶ Real Lives/Saving Lives: www.ciol.org.uk/real-lives. This scheme offers language practice in a series of practical, real-world scenarios that test your proficiency in a range of different languages: French, Spanish, German, Russian, Arabic, Mandarin, Welsh, ESOL, Polish and Somali. Suited to Year 9 and Year 10 students, this initiative could be of particular interest to students working towards their Duke of Edinburgh's Awards, or to those wishing to become St John Ambulance cadets.
- ▶ FluentU: www.fluentu.com/blog/language-moocs/. This immersive website brings language learning to life through

real-world videos. It also contains links to numerous free language learning websites as well as listing relevant job opportunities.

▶ Language learning MOOCs (massive open online courses): www.my-mooc.com/en/categorie/foreign-languages. This is an Aladdin's cave of different online language learning courses.

Social language projects

Hubs for people of any age and ability to practise their languages informally include the following.

▶ Meetup: Languages of London: www.meetup.com/Languages-of-London/. This is one of numerous networking sites that host events for those who want to meet others with an interest in languages.

▶ Yaketyyak: www.yaketyyak-languagecafe.co.uk/home. These language cafes are part of an initiative set up to provide venues in Edinburgh and Glasgow (and online) where people who want to chat with others in their chosen languages can meet up. French, Spanish, German, Italian, Portuguese, Mandarin, Japanese and Gaelic are currently available.

▶ Lingo Flamingo: www.lingoflamingo.co.uk. This is a Scottish initiative that uses language classes as a therapeutic tool for elderly patients at risk of dementia.

News and blogs

▶ Chartered Institute of Linguists: www.ciol.org.uk/news; www.ciol.org.uk/news/a-life-with-languages.

▶ *The Linguist*: https://blog.thelinguist.com.

▶ 'Life as a bilingual': www.psychologytoday.com/us/blog/life-bilingual; www.francoisgrosjean.ch/blog_en.html.

- ▶ Living Language: https://www.livinglanguage.com/blog/#.
- ▶ Cultural literacy: http://cleurope.eu/category/blog/.

Language reports and initiatives
- ▶ 'Languages for the future', British Council: www.britishcouncil.org/research-policy-insight/ policy-reports/languages-future-2017. This report provides a systematic analysis of the UK's language needs, taking economic, geopolitical, cultural and educational factors into consideration.
- ▶ The All-Party Parliamentary Group on Modern Languages: www.britishcouncil.org/education/schools/support-for-languages/thought-leadership/appg. This group runs campaigns and publishes documents to improve language policy in the UK as well as providing a parliamentary forum for the exchange of information.
- ▶ Healthy Linguistic Diet: http://healthylinguisticdiet.com. This site promotes learning languages as a form of mental exercise at any age. It's also possible to become active on the Healthy Linguistic Diet blog.
- ▶ Bilingualism Matters Centre: www.bilingualism-matters. ppls.ed.ac.uk. The centre's mission is to facilitate informed decision making on issues pertaining to bilingualism and to give access to up-to-date research evidence.
- ▶ PISA 2018 – Global Competence: www.oecd.org/pisa/pisa-2018-global-competence.htm. (See 'Competence, global' in the key concepts section that follows this chapter.)

Professional bodies
In linking cross-cultural communication with a good attitude and mutual respect, languages and language training can form a key part of corporate social responsibility. Many organizations have

internal communication departments, while others might supply (often outsourced) language training.

The list below contains the websites of a few professional bodies that give more information about courses and careers in which languages matter.

▶ Chartered Institute of Linguists: www.ciol.org.uk. The CIOL offers a Diploma in Translation (DipTrans) and a Diploma in Public Service Interpreting (DPSI); it also supports continuing development for newcomers to the profession.

▶ Language Services Direct: www.languageservicesdirect. co.uk. An organization that delivers language training for the public sector and for businesses.

▶ Communicaid: www.communicaid.com/clients/foreign-commonwealth-office-preparing-uk-diplomats-to-succeed-internationally/. The Foreign, Commonwealth & Development Office facilitates language training for diplomats in 70 languages, ranging from Arabic to Zulu.

Reources for readers interested in translation

▶ Institute of Translation and Interpreting: www.iti.org.uk

▶ International Association for Translation and Intercultural Studies: www.iatis.org/

▶ Globalization & Localization Association: www.gala-global. org/industry/industry-facts-and-data

▶ Translators without Borders: https:// translatorswithoutborders.org

Language research projects

▶ Language Acts and Worldmaking: www.languageacts.org. In their own words, this project 'aims to regenerate and transform modern language learning by foregrounding language's power to shape how we live and make our world'.

- ▶ Creative Multilingualism: www.creativeml.ox.ac.uk. Again in the initiative's own words: 'Activities that look into the creative dimension of languages, from cognition and production through to performance, translation and language learning.'
- ▶ Cross-Language Dynamics: Reshaping Community: http://projects.alc.manchester.ac.uk/cross-language-dynamics/. This is a programme 'exploring the relationship between language and community for the benefit of a more open world, and the role languages play in key issues such as social cohesion, health and diplomacy'.
- ▶ Multilingualism: Empowering Individuals, Transforming Societies: www.meits.org. MEITS is an organization that investigates how 'languages are vital for cultural understanding, social cohesion and wellbeing'. Its focus ranges from ' literature and film to education, linguistics and cognitive science'.

KEY CONCEPTS

What follows is a glossary of the key concepts of language learning and intercultural communication. As well as explaining each term, the list is also intended to demystify some of the ideas commonly encountered in the literature, on university courses, etc. The page numbers after the entries below point to places in the text where a concept or term is discussed.

Ab initio
A Latin term meaning 'from the beginning' that is often used in the descriptions of university language courses that start at the beginner's level.

Bilingual
The term 'bilingual' typically refers to a user of two languages, in contrast with 'multilingual', which applies to someone who uses three or more languages. Neurologically speaking, a multilingual's brain is known to be more complex than that of a bilingual. For the sake of simplicity, this book uses 'multilingual' as a generic term that includes 'bilingual'. (See pages 15, 32, 53, 54, 88.)

Common European Framework of Reference for Languages (CEFR)
An international standard for describing language ability. For more on this, see 'Language proficiency scales'. (See page 142.)

Competence, language

This is, basically, how well you speak a language. Our understanding about what constitutes (second) language competence has changed. Achieving functional ability in another language has come to replace a focus on 'native speaker competence'. Additionally, drawing on the components of different languages for communication purposes is seen as another form of language competence. See also 'Language proficiency scales' and 'Repertoire, language'. (See pages 59, 92, 94, 140, 176.)

Competence, global

This term isn't really about language per se. Instead it's about learning to understand and appreciate different cultural perspectives, in order to engage in open and effective interactions with people from different parts of the world (this is the Pisa 2018 definition). As we have seen, global competence can of course come about with increased language competence. (See pages 57, 58, 164.)

Content and Language Integrated Learning

An educational method with a 'dual-focused' objective. Here, selected subjects are taught through the medium of a particular target language (e.g. 'Mathematics through Spanish', for speakers of English). Essentially, this approach aims to enable students to deploy their acquired language skills in their future careers or studies. (See page 57.)

'Critical' period

This term has been used in proposing that there is a critical window in a young person's life for learning another language. But doing so later on isn't necessarily more difficult or effortful, it's just different, less spontaneous. In fact, we know that there is no cut-off age for learning another language. Children and adults learn languages in different ways: children learn more organically and instinctively, whereas adults learn more systematically. (See page 184; see also page 121.)

Education, 'well-rounded'
A curriculum that offers both STEM subjects (science, technology, engineering and mathematics) and SHAPE subjects (languages, literature, history, geography, economics). See also 'STEM' and 'SHAPE'. (See page 57.)

European Language Portfolio scheme
The ELP scheme is run by the Council of Europe. It is a flexible system of assessing a language learner's progress and is used especially for people who are on the move, measuring their progress in a particular language through ongoing formal testing and self-assessment. See also 'Common European Framework of Reference for Languages'. (See pages 80, 173.)

Language, easy/hard
You may sometimes be told that one language is harder to learn than another, but there is no single metric by which we can determine whether a language is difficult or straightforward to acquire. Perceived differences in difficulty have more to do with a learner's personal language background and their manner of engaging with the target language. (For 'easy', see pages 56, 156. For 'hard', see pages 56, 90, 157.)

Language, foreign
Many years ago, people studied 'foreign languages' at school and university. This notion is now seen as outdated, since many different languages are commonly spoken in any given country, but you may still find the term in use in some dark corner of the internet. The problem here is that the use of 'foreign' highlights the

distance between others' ways of life and cultures and our own. Many alternatives are commonly used, including in this book: another language, an additional language, a different language. (See pages 16, 23.)

Language, primary

This concept is used to describe the language a person uses most often. The notion of 'first language' can be a shifting target across a person's lifespan. Similarly, the concepts 'mother tongue' and 'native' language now tend to be seen as being too fixed for individuals in our world of heightened mobility, easy communication, sophisticated technology and cultural mixing. (See pages 36, 39, 51, 56, 61, 69, 102, 106, 108, 119, 141.)

Language proficiency scales

A standardized method of assessing a learner's language ability. Today's language proficiency certification procedures (as determined by the CEFR) measure a student's reading, listening, speaking and writing skills on a scale from A1 (a beginner) up to C2 (an advanced learner). See also 'European Language Portfolio Scheme' and 'Common European Framework of Reference for Languages (CEFR)'. (See pages 142, 143.)

Language, useful

A language's perceived worth in terms of its importance as a means of communication, or for other particular purposes. Such judgements about languages can be made on personal, social and/or economic grounds. (See pages 56, 150; see also pages 4, 14, 28.)

Lingua franca

An early-Italian expression used to describe a third language that serves as a means of communication between speakers who do not know each other's primary languages (e.g. speakers of French and Arabic using Spanish when interacting). (See page 42; see also 'trade language' on page 29.)

Linguist

This term can be confusing in the English language, as it describes two different types of people. In a narrow sense, a linguist is a (sometimes specially trained) person who draws on their skills in, or knowledge about, languages as a core part of their role in a business, a profession or in government. In a wider sense, the term is used for anyone who can use more than one language. (See pages 4, 78, 80.)

Monolingual

An individual is monolingual (or a monoglot) when they know only one language. This term is also used to describe countries that formally recognize only one official language (e.g. French in France). See also 'Polyglot/multilingual'. (See pages 15, 19, 20, 21, 32, 53, 54, 62.)

Motivation

An individual's external or internal drive: in this context, to learn another language. You may choose to undertake language learning as a means to an end – to get something that you consider worthwhile, such as employment – and/or you might want to be able to communicate with those around you or integrate into a new host society. Alternatively, you may tackle a fresh language purely for personal enrichment. (See pages 69, 110, 146.)

Polyglot/multilingual

Both 'polyglot' (from Greek *poly*, meaning many, and *glot*, meaning tongue) and 'multilingual' (from Latin *multi*, meaning many, and *lingua*, meaning language) describe people who know or can use several languages. A multilingual person may have been raised with several languages, whereas a polyglot would have learned them later. Relatedly, the term 'metrolingualism' describes the use of multilingual resources in urban spaces; various types of multilingualism are a social reality in every country. (For 'polyglot', see page 15. For 'multilingual', see pages 15, 22, 31–35, 50, 79, 81, 94, 101. Relatedly, the term 'metrolingualism' is discussed on page 36.)

Repertoire, language

Someone's 'language repertoire' describes their plurilingual competence. This could involve varying levels of proficiency in different languages and for different functions. An individual's repertoire can change over the course of their lifetime through acquisition of new languages. See also 'Competence, language'. (See pages 24, 113, 120.)

Resource, language

Someone who is able to speak more than one language has an additional resource they can draw on, and they are therefore able to do more in life. This can yield social rewards (e.g. greater social mobility) or economic benefits (e.g. a higher wage). An individual's bilingual skills can be a valued resource in the workplace. (See pages vi, 21, 38, 92, 109.)

Return on investment

A metric that uses a cost–benefit analysis on investment, e.g. in linking additional language skills with wage differentials. (See pages 56, 59.)

SHAPE

This recently coined acronym describes subjects that are not STEM subjects (see below). Standing for 'Social sciences, humanities and the arts for people and the economy', SHAPE subjects encompass everything from fine arts to economics, and they develop societal understanding and communication (or soft skills). (See page 57.)

Skills, hard/soft

A distinction is often made between 'hard' (technical) and 'soft' (interpersonal) skills. This book proposes that mastery in different languages is an essential (or key) skill, and it shows that soft skills often yield greater (professional) benefits when they are combined with a hard skill. (For 'hard', see page 148. For 'soft', see pages 85, 91, 97, 139, 148, 149.)

STEM

This acronym is shorthand for 'Science, technology, engineering, mathematics'. Some people instead use STEMM, which includes medicine. These subjects mainly develop technical abilities (often called hard skills). See also 'SHAPE'. (See pages 57, 134, 137, 145, 183.)

UCAS tariff points

These are used to translate your qualifications and grades into a numerical value for UK university entry requirements. Many qualifications (but not all) have a UCAS tariff value, which will vary depending on the particular qualification and the grade you achieved. (See page 135.)

ENDNOTES

This section contains references, additional comments and suggestions for further reading. All URLs are correct as of 18 January 2021.

1   This book is primarily intended for native speakers of English. You may of course have learned English later on, at school, and have another primary language, maybe because your parents use it at home or because you grew up using another language (either abroad or in the UK, speaking Welsh or Scots Gaelic, perhaps). In order to keep things simple, the main text does not refer to pre-existing individual bilingualism or multilingualism. I have, though, included an example of a more complex language trajectory: that of the author Jhumpa Lahiri, discussed in Chapters 4 and 6.

2   Fiction does have at least one famous Government Chief Linguist. In *Star Wars*, Jedi Master Jorus Trass served as Chief Linguist of the Almas Academy, an experimental Jedi academy located on Almas in the Cularin system. Among other films with a linguistic slant are *Arrival* and *The Interpreter*.

3   'A level French course': www.ashbournecollege.co.uk/a-level-college-london/a-level-courses/a-level-french-course.

4   'Sixth form Seville trip': www.liverpoolcollege.org.uk/parents-pupils/liverpool-college-news/807-sixth-form-seville-trip.

5   'James Freeman': www.bristol.ac.uk/sml/study/community/james-freeman.

6   'Meet our undegraduate students': www.ucl.ac.uk/european-languages-culture/programmes-courses/undergraduate/student-stories.

7   'Antony Fairclough': www.lancaster.ac.uk/languages-and-cultures/undergraduate/what-our-students-say/antony-fairclough.

8   'Japanese immersion: IEP student gains cultural appreciation': https://web.uri.edu/engineering/uncategorized/2020/01/uri-engineering-student-immerses-himself-in-japanese-culture-2

9   'Thomasina Miers: learning Spanish on a Mexican food odyssey – video': www.theguardian.com/education/video/2015/apr/02/thomasina-miers-learning-spanish-mexican-food-odyssey.

10 Miranda Moore, 2019, 'Being Frank: interview', *The Linguist*, 15 February (www.ciol.org.uk/being-frank).

11 'What does it feel like to speak and understand only one language?' (on Quora): http://bit.ly/39dw7Wq.

12 'What is it like to know just one language, how would you characterise ... your thoughts on languages generally, and what are your feelings toward multilingual people who either do or do not speak the language you do?' (on Quora): http://bit.ly/39bPNdo.

13 See note 11.

14 The YouGov stat pertaining to Americans can be found here: https://today. yougov.com/topics/lifestyle/articles-reports/2013/07/31/75-americans -have-no-second-language.

15 See note 14.

16 'Demand for bilingual workers more than doubled in 5 years, new report shows'. Press Release, *New American Economy*, 1 March 2017 (https://bit.ly/ 3orwrXo).

17 On language and trade across the ages, see G. Hogan-Brun, *Linguanomics: What Is the Market Potential of Multilingualism?* (Bloomsbury Academic, 2017).

18 On how we experience emotions in another language, see A. Pavlenko, *Emotions and Multilingualism* (Cambridge University Press, 2007).

19 For research evidence on how infants can already detect language differences, see J. C. Scott and A, M. E. Henderson, 2013, 'Language matters: thirteen-month olds understand that the language a speaker uses constrains conventionality', *Developmental Psychology* **49** (11), 2102–2211.

20 On Europeans and their languages, see 'Special Eurobarometer, European Commission, 2012': https://ec.europa.eu/commfrontoffice/publicopinion/ archives/ebs/ebs_386_en.pdf.

21 For more detailed information see 'London's second languages mapped by tube stop'. *The Guardian*, 30 October 2014 (http://bit.ly/3npsIsR).

22 'Language in England and Wales: 2011', Office for National Statistics (http:// bit.ly/2LrfoqA).

23 For more information on the promotion of multilingualism in urban areas, see the Eurocities website (www.eurocities.eu) and 'Multilingualism in education – bilingual learners' (www.languagescompany.com/wp-content/upl oads/14_1132-LUC_Toolkit_Plurilingual_V5 Online.pdf).

24 'Survival International': www.survivalinternational.org.

25 'Scots Gaelic could die out within a decade, study finds': Severin Carrell, *The Guardian*, 2 July 2020 (http://bit.ly/3nptqq1).

26 'Atlas of the World's languages in danger': www.unesco.org/languages-atlas/.

27 Albert Costa and Núria Sebastián-Gallés, 2014, 'How does the bilingual experience sculpt the brain?', *Nature Reviews Neuroscience* **15**(5), 336–345.

28 Andrea Mechelli *et al.*, 2004, 'Structural plasticity in the bilingual brain', *Nature* **431**, 757.

29 'Bilinguals of two spoken languages have more gray matter than monolinguals': *Science Daily*, 16 July 2015 (http://bit.ly/2LaaVc6).

30 Voncent DelLuca, Katrien Segaert, Ali Mazaheri and Andrea Krott, 2020, 'Understanding bilingual brain function and structure changes? U bet! A unified bilingual experience trajectory model', *Journal of Neurolinguistics* **56**, 100930 (http://bit.ly/2Irh9nG).

31 Albert Costa, *The Bilingual Brain: And What It Tells Us About the Science of Language*, translated by John Schwieter (Allen Lane, London, 2020).

32 O. A. Olulade *et al.*, 2015, 'Neuroanatomical evidence in support of the bilingual advantage theory', *Cerebral Cortex*, 16 July.

33 Ferris Jabr, 2011, 'Cache cab: taxi drivers' brains grow to navigate London's streets', *Scientific American: Mind*, 8 December (http://bit.ly/3hQN90x).

34 Katherine Wollett, Hugo Spiers and Eleanor Maguire, 'Talent in the taxi: a model system for exploring expertise', *Philosophical Transactions of the Royal Society B: Biological Sciences* **364**(1522), 1407–1416 (https://bit.ly/3bdZ9rT).

35 Gaia Vince, 2016, 'The amazing benefits of being bilingual', *BBC Future*, 12 August (http://bbc.in/3hQNtfL).

36 'Pisa Global Competence Framework': www.oecd.org/pisa/pisa-2018-global-competence.htm.

37 Sophie Hardach, 2018, 'Speaking more than one language can boost economic growth', *World Economic Forum*, 6 February (http://bit.ly/3buhAsz). Further evidence on the increased earning potential of bilinguals comes from Albert Saiz and Elena Zoido, 2005, 'Listening to what the world says: bilingualism and earnings in the US', *Review of Economics and Statistics* **87**(3), 523–538.

38 Jacek Liwiński, 2019, 'The wage premium from foreign language skills', *Empirica* **46**, 691–711.

39 This graph, created by John Hogan, is based on comparative empirical research data from Liwiński (2019) and Saiz and Zoido (2005). Using an earnings multiplier, it shows that, for example, the earnings of Polish–French intermediate bilinguals are more than 1.8 times higher than those of their monolingual counterparts after five years.

40 'Graduate outcomes: provider level data', 25 June 2020, from the GOV.UK website (http://bit.ly/2JT3Dc9).

41 See note 9. Extracts: my transcript.

42 Jhumpa Lahiri, 2016, 'I am, in Italian, a tougher, a freer writer', *The Observer* (New Review), 31 January, 16–18.

43 See note 10.

44 Martina Navratilova, 2020, 'Learning multiple languages helped me on the court and in life', *The Independent* (Long Read), 3 February (http://bit.ly/2MJDBsT).

45 Miranda Moore, 2017, 'The final frontier: interview', *The Linguist*, 28 April (www.ciol.org.uk/final-frontier).

46 Quoted in 'European Space Agency: we have to learn many languages, like Chinese', 2018, *CGTN.COM*, 28 June (http://bit.ly/2XlEkSZ).

47 See the creative multilingualism research project: www.creativeml.ox.ac.uk.

48 P. L. McGroarty, 2019, '*Outlander*'s Fergus grows up: all eyes on French actor Romann Berrux', *internationalfilmreview*, 14 December (https://internationalfilmreview.net/tag/fergus-outlander/).

49 Ariston Anderson, 2014, 'Venice: Viggo Mortensen talks mastering new languages', *Hollywood Reporter*, 9 February (http://bit.ly/3bdHEYF).

50 Mark Savage, 2019, 'Sofia Reyes: meet Mexico's multilingual pop sensation', *BBC News*, 4 April (http://bbc.in/3bjat66).

51 W. Morris and T. Anderson, 2019, 'Game of Thrones: speak Dothraki like Daenerys with our handy guide', *BBC News*, 12 April (http://bbc.in/38l1kYE); my transcript. See also the website of the Language Creation Society: https://gameofthrones.fandom.com/wiki/David_J._Peterson.

52 Personal communication, 7 October 2020.

53 On Esperanto speakers, see *Ethnologue*: www.ethnologue.com.

54 See the video footage embedded in 'Coach and 12 missing boys found alive in flooded cave in Thailand', *The Irish Times*, 2 July 2018 (http://bit.ly/3ou96W0).

55 Derina Johnson, 2018, 'Adul Sam-on: the stateless boy who survived the Thai cave – and helped with the rescue', *The Conversation*, 13 July (http://bit.ly/3s5qbr8).

56 See 'Top bilingual jobs in 2021' on Cudoo: https://cudoo.com/blog/top-trending-jobs-for-bilingual-speakers-in-2021

57 Lu-Hai Liang, 2013, 'Language graduates: what jobs are they doing now?', *The Guardian* (The Case for Language Learning), 16 October (http://bit.ly/3burdrd).

58 Career statistics are from http://careers-advice-online.com/career-change-statistics.html.

59 This diplomat's name has been changed. Many thanks go to the real 'Josh', with whom I had a telephone conversation on 1 October 2020.

60 See note 57.

61 G. Lüdi, 2014, 'Dynamics and management of linguistic diversity in companies and institutions of higher education. Results from the DYLAN-project', in *Plurilingual Education, Policies – Practices – Language Development*, ed. P Grommes and A. Hu, pp. 113–138 (J. Benjamins, Amsterdam).

62 'Competing across borders: how cultural and communication barriers affect business', *Economist Intelligence Report: Perspectives*, 25 April, 2012 (http://bit.ly/2L3F2SD).

63 Matthew Reisz, 2014, 'Language degrees: when the words are not enough', *Times Higher Education*, 11 December.

64 Her real name has been changed.

65 'Asda offers "free alcohol" in wrong Welsh translation', *BBC News*, 17 April 2017 (http://bbc.in/3ooRV89).

66 'List of multilingual bands and artists', Wikipedia (http://bit.ly/3bsic1s).

67 '13 gifted K-Pop idols who may speak your native language', Koreaboo blog post, 15 March 2019 (http://bit.ly/39bZhFJ).

68 Luna-Anastasia Riedel, 2020, 'K-Pop as a linguistic phenomenon', *Diggit Magazine*, 9 March (http://bit.ly/3nrjBIe).

69 You can read about the profiles of these young artists in a report titled 'Slanguages in the creative economy' from June 2020: https://bit.ly/38nD9c2.

70 Lucy Jeynes, 2013, 'STEM subjects versus the arts: why languages are just as important', *The Guardian* (Women in Leadership), 6 September (http://bit.ly/2LdxUTF).

71 See note 42.

72 Jhumpa Lahiri, 2016, *In Altre Parole*, p. 21 (Tascabili Guanda, Milan) (my translation).

73 Lahiri (2016, p. 23).

74 This is from a video clip titled 'In the studio: Jhumpa Lahiri on how learning Italian transformed her life', available on the Penguin Random House Audio Publishing blog (http://bit.ly/3hTMA6g).

75 See note 45.

76 See note 46.

77 See note 44.

78 Lauren Collins, 2016, *When in French: Love in a Second Language* (Harper Collins: 4th Estate).

79 Personal communication from Gowri Joharatnam and Nalinie Joharatnam (6 June 2020).

80 More information on Sir Richard Burton is available in the article 'Great explorers: Victorian polyglot and eroticist who, disguised as a merchant, tricked his way into Mecca (which almost cost him his life)', *The Guardian*, 2 May 2020. Burton supposedly spoke 29 (European, Asian and African)

languages and famously translated *Arabian Nights* (originally entitled *Thousand Nights and a Night*) into English.

81 Richard Burton, quoted in Thomas Wright, 1906, *The Life of Sir Richard Burton*, chapter II (October 1840–April 1842) (Everett, London). This chapter was rendered into HTML by Steve Thomas for the University of Adelaide Library in 2003 and is available at http://bit.ly/38rkLPA.

82 For more nuanced information on second language learning, see, for example, V. Cook, 2016, *Second Language Learning and Language Teaching*, 5th edn (Routledge).

83 Lahiri (2016, p. 23) (my translation).

84 Jhumpa Lahiri, 2015, 'Teach yourself Italian', *The New Yorker*, 30 November (http://bit.ly/2LcnlQI).

85 See note 84.

86 See note 45.

87 See note 44.

88 See note 84.

89 Lahiri (2016); Jhumpa Lahiri, 2017, *In Other Words*, translated by Ann Goldstein (Bloomsbury).

90 See note 74.

91 See note 46.

92 See note 45.

93 On bilingualism and additional language learning, see University of Haifa, 2011, 'Bilinguals find it easier to learn a third language', *ScienceDaily*, 1 February (http://bit.ly/39fuI1B).

94 Healthy Linguistic Diet: http://healthylinguisticdiet.com. See also T. H. Bak and D. Mehmedbegovic, 2017, 'Healthy linguistic diet: the value of linguistic diversity and language learning across the lifespan', *Languages, Society and Policy*, Policy Paper, 21 May (www.repository.cam.ac.uk/handle/1810/264363).

95 D. Mehmedbegovic, 2018, 'What every policymaker needs to know about cognitive benefits of bilingualism', In *Languages after Brexit*, ed. M. Kelly, pp. 109–124 (Palgrave Macmillan).

96 There is ample research evidence showing that age does not limit an individual's ability to learn a new language. While some debate exists on whether there is a period that is 'critical' to language learning – as well as on when this period would begin and how long it might last – this 'critical period' does not equate to a 'cut-off age'. On life-long language learning, see E. Bialystok, Fergus I. M. Craik and Morris Freedman, 2007, 'Bilingualism as a protection against the onset of symptoms of dementia', *Neuropsychologia* **45**(2), 459–464.

97 Part of this chapter draws on information provided in the QAA Benchmark Statement for Languages, Cultures and Societies (December 2019), where further information can be found: https://bit.ly/38q0Alh.

98 'Getting "real" – a new challenge for language learners', part of the 'Real lives' language project for schools from the Chartered Institute of Linguists (https://bit.ly/3hXxxsq).

99 Issues relating to the financing of higher education are in flux, and the situation is completely different in Scotland, so make sure you update yourself on the Augar Review: 'Post-18 review of education and funding: independent panel report'. See also Abby Young-Powell, 2019, 'How much should parents pay for university?', *The Guardian*, 9 July (http://bit.ly/3nz4dcZ.)

100 On language proficiency (self-) assessment see: www.coe.int/en/web/common-european-framework-reference-languages/level-descriptions.

101 From 1 January 2021, when the UK fully left the European Union, the UK government will no longer participate in the EU Erasmus⁺ scheme (unless you live in Northern Ireland: see www.bbc.co.uk/news/uk-northern-ireland-55455532). At the time of writing (5 January 2021), details of a new UK-funded scheme, intended to enable students to study at universities all over the world and named after the mathematician Alan Turing, have yet to be announced.

102 See note 45.

103 A link to graduate destinations can be found on the UCAS website: www.ucas.com/explore/subjects/languages. See also footnote 104 for more information about programmes and careers in languages.

104 For more information visit the websites of the Chartered Institute of Linguists (CIOL) and the Institute of Translation and Interpreting (ITI). These organizations provide regulated qualifications for aspiring language professionals.

105 On the importance of languages for defence/peacekeeping purposes, see the British Academy's *Lost for Words* (www.thebritishacademy.ac.uk/publications/lost-words-need-languages-uk-diplomacy-and-security/).

ABOUT THE AUTHOR

GABRIELLE HOGAN-BRUN is a currently a visiting professor and senior researcher at Vytautas Magnus University in Kaunas, having previously taught at the Universities of Bristol and Basel. She lectures widely on language attitudes, policies and practices, and on economic aspects of multilingualism. She serves on several international journal editorial boards and has worked with various European organizations on matters of language diversity.

A Salzburg Global Fellow, she is a co-author of the Salzburg Statement for a Multilingual World. She is the founding book series editor of Palgrave Studies in Minority Languages and Communities, and co-editor of *The Palgrave Handbook of Minority Languages and Communities* (2019), which won the BAAL book prize (in 2020). Among her other recent publications is *Linguanomics: What Is the Market Potential of Multilingualism?* (Bloomsbury Academic, 2017).

Why Study
HISTORY?

Marcus Collins
Peter N. Stearns

"This book is a breath of fresh air! If you're wondering about whether to study history at university, whether it's a practical choice, what job you might get at the end of it, and how to choose where to study, this is the book for you."

— Suzannah Lipscomb, Professor of History, University of Roehampton

"A brilliant guide to choosing the right course, from the type of history on offer to selecting the institution best suited to you. I recommend it to all students and their parents as they plan their next steps."

— Holly Hiscox, history teacher, d'Overbroeck's Sixth Form, Oxford

"An excellent guide for students of history ... This short guide busts a lot of myths and offers practical advice based on an unparalleled understanding of how history is actually taught on both sides of the Atlantic."

— Peter Mandler, University of Cambridge

"At last, we have a volume that directly challenges the doubts and apprehensions many students have about studying history. Much needed and highly recommended."

— Robert B. Townsend, American Academy of Arts and Sciences

Why Study
MATHEMATICS?

Vicky Neale

"An insightful guide for anyone considering studying mathematics at university. It ... highlights the wide variety of career options that a maths degree opens up [and] includes important examples of where maths is used in the real world."

— Nicholas J. Higham, Richardson Professor of Applied Mathematics, University of Manchester

"An essential read for anyone considering studying mathematics at university. Vicky Neale takes you through what to expect in your studies, and explains the practical uses and beauty of a mathematics degree."

— James Grime, lecturer, public speaker and *Numberphile* presenter

"Detailed, accessible and broad ranging, this book refines the complex and varying nature of high-level mathematics into a useful and relatable form. An ideal guide for A level maths students when pondering their next steps."

— Kerry Burnham, headteacher, Exeter Maths School

"I highly recommend this book to any student, including those who are exploring their university options and those who are already set on a mathematics degree and want to explore the implications of their choice."

— Dr Jamie Frost, founder of DrFrostMaths and Top 10 Finalist for the Global Teacher Prize 2020

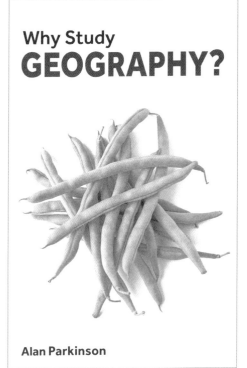

Why Study GEOGRAPHY?

Alan Parkinson

Studying any subject at degree level is an investment in the future that involves significant cost. Now more than ever, students and their parents need to weigh up the potential benefits of university courses. That's where the *Why Study* series comes in. This series of books, aimed at students, parents and teachers, explains in practical terms the range and scope of an academic subject at university level and where it can lead in terms of careers or further study. Each book sets out to enthuse the reader about its subject and answer the crucial questions that a college prospectus does not.

London Publishing Partnership is pleased to offer discounts to educational establishments that wish to buy either a full set of books from the series or multiple copies of a single book. We also sell sets of the books at a discounted price to people wishing to donate them to a school, sixth form college or university, or to institutions wishing to buy copies to distribute to students and/or teachers to promote a particular subject.

Anyone wishing to find out more can email us on
lpp@londonpublishingpartnership.co.uk